TO VICTORIA, BROOKLYN, ROMEO, AND CRUZ, MY WIFE AND MY
BOYS, YOU MAKE THIS ALL SO MUCH MORE SPECIAL FOR ME.
YOUR SUPPORT, YOUR HONESTY AND, MOST IMPORTANTLY FOR
ME, YOUR LOVE MEANS SO MUCH. I LOVE YOU ALL.

TO MY MUM AND DAD, SISTERS, NAN AND GRANDAD,
YOU HAVE ALL GIVEN ME SO MUCH LOVE, SUPPORT, AND
STRENGTH. I WOULD NOT BE IN THIS POSITION WITHOUT
YOU ALL. YOU HAVE MADE ME WHAT I AM TODAY.

TO ANY BOY OR GIRL READING THIS, I HOPE YOU FIND
INSPIRATION AND GO ON TO REALIZE YOUR DREAMS.
BELIEVE IN YOURSELF, WORK HARD, AND YOU WILL GO FAR.

FINALLY, TO ALL OF MY FANS, WITHOUT YOU I WOULDN'T BE
WHERE I AM TODAY.

DAVID

_DAVID BECKHAM'S
SOCCER SKILLS

Collins

An Imprint of HarperCollinsPublishers

First published in the UK in 2006 by
HarperSport, an imprint of
HarperCollinsPublishers London

Collins is an imprint of HarperCollins Publishers.

David Beckham's Soccer Skills

Library of Congress Catalog Card Number is
available.

ISBN-13: 978-0-06-115475-1
ISBN-10: 0-06-115475-X

Design and Art Direction by 'OMEDESIGN

Photography by mooneyphoto with the exception
of pages 22, 23, 24, 25, 26, 27, 46, 47, 48, 49
(courtesy of David Beckham) and pages 10, 11, 51,
61, 82, 94, 106, 107, 121, 128, 130, 135, 139, 141, 143,
145(x1), 149, 150, 155 (x2) (Getty Images)

Acknowledgments

First and foremost, I would like to thank all the coaches and staff at The Los
Angeles Academy for all their hard work and dedication. Particularly Mo
Boreham, Betsy Pollard, Steve Myles, and Michael Quigley. Also a special thanks
to Bill Peterson.

I would also like to thank all the staff at The London Academy. Especially
Eric, Ted, and Gary, whose invaluable insight to the game has contributed so
much.

To Terry, thank you for all your support and advice. You were instrumental
in the realization of my dream and continue to be an integral part of the reality.

A special thanks to Simon Fuller for making the dream come true.
Thanks for always being there; your continued support means so much.

Thanks to George, Harley, Ashleigh, Riana, James, and Louis for your
participation in the photo shoot for the book. You showed great enthusiasm and
were all fantastic. Thanks also to all the children who participated at the launch.

To the team at HarperCollins, including Michael, Tom, Jane, Sarah, and
Eleanor, it's been great working with you again. Particular thanks to Leo
Moynihan, for all your hard work.

To Jilly and Martin at 'OME DESIGN, thanks for your terrific design work.

To all my friends at 19 Entertainment, especially James, Suzy, Maya, Ceara,
Simon O, Nez, Niki, Grenville, and Zach.

To Simon Mooney, Julian & Ed at mooneyphoto for their superb photography.

Thanks to Anschutz Entertainment Group and The Academy partners; adidas,
Volkswagen, and Motorola, as well as all at Lee & Thompson.

Thanks, as well, to all the great players I've been privileged to play alongside
at Manchester United, Real Madrid, and England. Whatever I've done has only
been possible because of the talent, commitment, and inspiration of the other ten.

INTRODUCTION   7

_01 GETTING PREPARED   8
    THE ACADEMY_ AIM AND VISION   18
    CHILDHOOD DREAMS   22

_02 BALL CONTROL   28
    THE ACADEMY_ CONCEPT   38

_03 MAKING SPACE   42
    LIVING THE DREAM   46

_04 TURNING   52
    THE ACADEMY_ STAFF AND SET-UP   66

_05 PASSING   68
    SO MANY MEMORIES   84

_06 DRIBBLING   90
    THE ACADEMY_ THE PROGRAMS   96

_07 DEFENDING   102
    THE ACADEMY_ THE CLASSROOM   108
    MORE THAN A SOCCER PLAYER   112

_08 CROSSING   118
    IT'S ALL IN THE CLEATS   130

_09 FINISHING   132
    ON THE WORLD STAGE   142

_10 FREE KICKS AND PENALTIES   146
    PARENTS, KIDS, AND TEACHERS   156

    FACTFILE   158

_CONTENTS

Soccer has taught me a lot. During my time in the game I have had to learn how to deal with the highs and the lows, the triumphs and the setbacks. It's been quite a journey and one that I hope still has a fair few twists and turns. You're never quite sure of what is around the corner, but what I am certain of is that I wouldn't change a thing.

This book takes a look at that journey, but it is about much more than that. On these pages I hope you will get a sense of what has gone into making the dreams of a young boy become reality. I have always said that I'm no coach and that I have no intentions of becoming one when my playing days are over, but I feel I can pass on what I have learned and hopefully help the next generation grasp the basics of a sport that has been so good to me and one I will always love.

A large section of this book strives to do just that. Be it crossing the ball, taking that vital free kick, or even defending, you'll find my tips on how to do it inside. You may not be the best player, but that doesn't matter; all you need is the will to improve and the enthusiasm to go with it.

There comes a time in every player's life—no matter how illustrious his career has been—when he asks himself what he will do next. From early on in my career I knew that I wanted to give aspiring kids the opportunity to realize their dreams, and I came up with a plan to open soccer academies for kids all around the world.

That dream has today become a reality, and my Academy is now "open for business." We're all very proud of what we have achieved. There is nothing like seeing kids come to us and not only learn but have a wonderful time. We have the best coaches working in facilities that are second to none, and in these pages you will get a taste of what is going on, on a daily basis, in our little corner of South-East London and beyond.

My own "daily basis" still involves getting up, going to training, and preparing for soccer games. I have the same enthusiasm for the game today at Real Madrid as I did when I first started out as a young hopeful at Manchester United.

As I say, it's been quite a journey and I hope you enjoy the ride.

_INTRODUCTION

1

GETTING PREPARED_

Warming up and getting prepared for action is a huge part of the modern game, as is warming down and recovering from the activity, be it a training session or a game. If you ask most soccer players, though, they won't tell you that they enjoy warming up and I'm afraid I'm the same. I'd rather just get into training but, over time, I have learned that you cannot do that and risk injury. Most players know that warming up is an imperative part of playing the game.

Warming up and stretching is massively important and it is vital that players do it right. I don't think it should be for too long, though. It should be short and sharp, consisting of good stretches, good exercises, and some good sprint work. It's not until you have played at this level for a while that you

realize just how important a good warm-up is.

The same goes for warming down. This has also become a vital part of a soccer player's game. In training I'd much rather keep practicing my free kicks or shooting, but I get dragged over and I have to join in the warm-down.

It is important that after a hard session or a game itself that you let the body slowly warm down. There was a time when players would just jump into a bath, but today it is important that we do some light running and stretching before relaxing in our Jacuzzis.

When it comes to warming up, I think it would be wise if I let Gary Lewin, the Arsenal and England physical therapist, describe how to plan both a good warm-up and warm-down. On the England squad we all listen to what he has to say, so I suggest you do too. Over to you, Gary.

David's quite right when he says that most professionals don't like to warm up. He loves soccer—that's clear to anyone who's seen him train and play. The thing is, like so many others, he hates warming up!

I have yet to meet a player who enjoys it. Pros don't like it, kids don't like it, and you can understand why. They want to get on with playing soccer. Running around for ten minutes, stretching for ten minutes, and sprinting for ten minutes can seem like a waste of valuable playing time, but it is important that you learn from a young age that a good warm-up is crucial as a way of both getting the body ready for immediate action and preventing long-term injuries.

It sounds obvious but what you have to do before you start playing is literally warm the body up. When you are inactive, most of your blood is going to your main organs. When you start exercising, you are going to need that blood to transfer to your muscles and that is going to take time.

Make the body work at a low intensity so the muscles start working and therefore the heart is nicely pumping and blood can go where it is most needed. The blood will go from the main organs to the muscle groups and therefore supply them with the vital nutrients that they need in order for them to work and be at their most effective.

When you get out of bed in the morning, your balance is not at its best, your perception is not as sharp as later in the day, and your concentration is not good. As the day progresses, your body and your mind wake up, and warming up is simply an athlete's way of waking up the body and preparing it for the task ahead.

Physiologically, your mind also becomes sharper, your brain gets active, your balance mechanisms start kicking in, and your body is getting prepared for the game. Basically you are preparing yourself for activity.

If you have switched the mind onto the fact that

"A GOOD WARM-UP IS CRUCIAL AS A WAY OF BOTH GETTING THE BODY READY FOR IMMEDIATE ACTION AND PREVENTING LONG-TERM INJURIES."

you are about to carry out rigorous exercise, your balance will have improved and you are less likely to injure yourself by doing the wrong thing such as slipping over the ball. It sounds silly, but the need to be ready for action is that vital.

The reasons why you warm up professional soccer players is because they are finely tuned athletes. Kids are different. They are already naturally very active, and so it is a gray area when talking about how best to warm them up.

The main thing to emphasize is that you get used to warming up before you play a game or a training session. You then have a really solid base, and when you get older, it becomes the normal thing to do and you are then more used to preparing yourself mentally and physically for the task ahead.

If you go to kick a ball and you are stiff, that muscle is far more likely to strain, pull, or even tear. By warming up you are reducing that risk. The ideal warm-up will prepare you physically, and mentally, for what is about to happen.

_GARY LEWIN

WARM-UP FOR TRAINING

Warming up for a training session is far more difficult. There is no end goal, no game situation to get fired up for, so it can be hard to get players going. Try to make sure that you have some technical skills added to the warm-up. If you incorporate some ball work, as far as motivation goes you will see the benefits. Involve the ball; keep the interest as well as tuning the body into what is to come.

Ten or fifteen years ago you wouldn't touch a ball for the first half an hour, but now we recognize how important it is to utilize the ball within a warm-up. At a low intensity level, use the ball, as it allows the player to warm up mentally when he or she has the ball at their feet.

WARM-UP FOR GAME

Once you are in game mode, the warm-up is much more focused. You are getting ready for the game and therefore are that much more switched on. The intensity is already there.

"THE IDEAL WARM-UP WILL PREPARE YOU PHYSICALLY AND MENTALLY."

A GOOD WARM-UP
INITIAL MOVEMENT

Start with some light jogging. This simply gets the blood pumping around the body. Pros will run around in twos and usually that is their time to chat and catch up. With kids it is nice to utilize games to make the warm-up a bit more fun.

The coach can have the kids running around and shout out instructions, such as touch the floor, change direction, get into groups of three and then four. You get the concentration going and the players become gradually focused.

STATIC STRETCHES
FOR 5 OR 6 MINUTES

These work on each main muscle group. Make sure you carry out a slow and gradual stretch, not a bounce, as that can cause injury. Make sure your body weight is over the limb you're stretching. Keep your body upright; don't lean into the stretch, as the limb won't feel the benefits. Feel the stretch and hold it.

Work on the following areas:
_The Calf
_The Hamstring
  (that is, the back of the leg from the knee up)
_The Quads
  (that is, the top front of the leg from the knee up)
_The Groin
_The Hips
_The Back
_The Neck

Static stretches still have their place, but make sure you don't overdo it.

STRETCHING
DYNAMIC STRETCHES

There was a time when stretching was purely static and involved a slow stretch that would work only one muscle group. Dynamic stretching is different. It incorporates a pattern of movement rather than one stretch, and should involve two or three muscle groups. This form of stretching is actually much more functional to soccer and to sports. When you stretch for a ball, you are not only working the hamstring, the thigh, or the calf, you can be working all three, so it is imperative to have all the different muscles fired as well as improving coordination of the limb to the brain.

Try these dynamic stretches:

_Kick diagonally across the body to warm up those legs.

_Open the gate.
This involves stretching the leg out, taking it, bent at the knee from the inside, out.

_Close the gate.
This is obviously the opposite, as we take the leg from the outside, in.

_Heel flicks.
While lightly jogging, flick your heels up to your backside.

_Knee raises.
Again, jogging lightly, bring your knees up to waist height.

_Skipping.
This is a great way of getting that heart pumping.

Up the pace, make the strides a bit bigger, bring in a few jumps, a few skips, twists, and turns. Get the breathing going and make sure the cardiovascular and the respiratory centers are really going. You should have a nice glow on by now.

You can finish with some ball work and then gradually go into the more intense soccer work.

It is important that you take on board these good habits, but science has proved that you don't need to do too much with warm-ups. The stretching after games can be just as, or even more, vital.

Dynamic stretching is a relatively new technique, but it aids the preparation process.

It's all in the preparation. Be sure to work all the major muscle groups. That's the groin, the hamstring, the quads, and the calf.

WARM-DOWNS

Players hate warm-downs too. They'd much rather shower and go home. If you can, however, get used to it at a young age, it becomes normal.

Basically, in a warm-down you are carrying out the warm-up but in reverse. The exercises you do in the warm-down gradually get slower rather than faster until you are eventually walking.

Slowly jog until you finish with a walk.

As for stretching, you start in a full stretch but bring that movement down so it is less and less. By pumping the blood around further, you are getting rid of the toxins in the muscles, and instead of just suddenly stopping—which allows lactic acid to get into the muscle—you are flushing it through at a very low intensity.

David, like other players, may not enjoy this process; however, they all understand how important it is. He loves training; he loves working at his game and is very dedicated to his job. He is also very skillful, there's no doubt about that, but what people don't see is the hard work he puts in behind the scenes. Even after so many years and so much success, he is still working on his game. You'll always see him practicing his free kicks, every day, rain or shine. It doesn't matter how good you are—you need to practice.

He hasn't (knock on wood) had too many injuries. He has had a few problems with his back, but we know that is postural and that those problems are caused simply by the incredible positions he gets into to strike the ball and achieve the movement in the ball that causes keepers so much trouble.

David believes that if you prepare properly with the correct warm-up and warm-down, you can reduce the number of injuries that your body could sustain.

You may want to go straight into the shower, but it's vital you warm down after any match or training session.

"DAVID TAKES CARE OF HIMSELF SO WELL THAT HE RARELY GETS INJURED."

When I was eight years old, it was rare to find me doing anything other than playing soccer. All I needed was a ball and some space. Friends would join in, but if none were around, that was no problem—I would play alone. It was as simple as that. A park, a street, my yard, a playground, a field: These were all places where I could play the game I had grown to love. The game I knew I would play when I grew up.

Having said all that, I would have loved somewhere to go to play and learn, somewhere organized with the best coaches, great facilities, and all the space a kid could dream of. Back when I was a child, we could play out in the park until dark. All-day games were the norm, but today kids just don't do that. The world has changed. Streets and parks can be dangerous places and parents—of which I am one—want their kids somewhere out of harm's way.

That's why I wanted to open a soccer academy. I wanted to create a dream place for kids that also helped them get off the streets. I wanted somewhere that would be fun and educational, a place they could enjoy safely.

THE ACADEMY:
AIM AND VISION_

I guess that by now, you will have realized that as a child I was absolutely soccer-crazy. I still am, I guess. The posters may have come down from my bedroom walls, but I still love the game with a passion. Back then, though, Manchester United was everything to me. I may have lived miles away from my heroes, but that obsession for the team that my dad had spent hours on end telling me about soon reached a fever pitch.

One afternoon I was watching television and I saw that Bobby Charlton was running a soccer school and it was based in Manchester. I just knew that I had to be there. Bobby Charlton! A player my dad had told me all about and a man who had done so much, both as a player and an ambassador, to make his team and his country famous all around the world. A legend.

It was my granddad who paid for me to go to Manchester for what was an incredible experience. The memories from the great man's school will always be with me. Of course, I always wanted to

"IT'S AMAZING WHAT
THE SOCCER WORLD
CAN BRING TO KIDS
AND HOW IT CAN
MAKE THEM FEEL."

play for Manchester United, so to see that there was a soccer school in Manchester was for me a dream come true. I went there, age ten, and it was great. I loved it and so I went again the following year, and being a year older it was that much better. I won the competition that year too, which made it extra special and enabled me to meet heroes such as Mark Hughes and Bryan Robson.

Bobby was down there a lot, which was great, but so were many of the players from United, who would come along, answer questions, pose for photos, and sign autographs. These guys were my idols and to meet them in the flesh was the best. Kids love to see their heroes; they'll go home, they'll tell their parents and their friends, and that's special. It's amazing what the soccer world can bring to kids and how it can make them feel. Now that I am from that soccer world, it's important for me to give something back and my reward is seeing the joy on so many kids' faces.

I look back on my two summers with Bobby Charlton with such fond memories and now I want to do the same for today's children. I want to create memories, memories that will last forever. I didn't want to create just a soccer school. I wanted a place that was about more than just soccer and how you enjoy it. It's important to me that kids can come here and do more than show their talent. I want them to enjoy the game, learn about the game, and take in just how much soccer—whether or not you are good at it—can bring to your life.

What inspired me to create my Academy was the reward I get from seeing children truly enjoy themselves in a professional soccer environment. I've been to other schools and academies as a guest and you see the look on the faces of the children when a professional player—maybe a hero of some of those kids—comes along. It is an amazing buzz to see that happiness from something so simple and I wanted to create that. You can't buy that feeling and

that's why I have started my own Academy.

Now that it's up and running, my vision for The Academy is to make it even bigger and even more impressive than it already is. At the moment it's starting up and people like what they see. My vision in five years is for me to be closely involved in the day-to-day running of the place and to expand so we have as many schools as possible all around the world.

"WHAT INSPIRED ME TO CREATE THE DAVID BECKHAM ACADEMY WAS THE REWARD I GET FROM SEEING CHILDREN TRULY ENJOY THEMSELVES IN A PROFESSIONAL SOCCER ENVIRONMENT."

"**M**um, mum," I said, pulling at her skirt. At first she ignored me, but I persevered. "Mum!" Finally she looked down, wondering what all the fuss was about. "Mum, I'm going to be the captain of England when I grow up."

Don't ask me at what age I realized I wanted to be a professional soccer player. I've asked my parents and even they don't recall how old I was when I started telling everyone that I was going to play the game for a living. I think it's always been there. All I ever wanted to do was to play soccer, and to play it for Manchester United and my country.

When I bothered my mum as a young boy, she would give me a knowing look as if to say, that's nice, David, now go and play. Of course, lots of children grow up with that very wish: that they are going to be a pro soccer player and captain for their country. It's a desire all fans grow up with, and to this day I realize just how unbelievably lucky I have been, in that every one of my dreams I had as that boy annoying his busy mum has ultimately come true.

From becoming a professional soccer player and playing for Manchester United, through wearing their number 7 shirt and playing alongside Bryan Robson, and then to playing for England and eventually captaining my country's team—look, Mum, I did it. I've been able to achieve all those dreams, and I never take that for granted. It's taken a little more than just dreaming, though; along the way there's been a lot of hard work.

That was drilled into me from a young age. My dad never stopped telling me that you don't get anywhere without putting in hours and hours of work. Advice like that from your dad can sound a little boring, but it was the best advice I could have

received as an aspiring young player. My mum and dad have always had that ethos. We had a good size yard, not a big one but long, and I would go to the far end and work on keeping the ball up and there I'd stay.

Practice, practice, practice, for hours.

With my dad in my ear, that practice made perfect and you could always find him and me over at the park kicking a ball at each other. I just wanted to shoot at him and score, but he worked on all aspects of my game, especially ball control and passing using my weaker left foot.

To put it simply, if you don't work hard, you won't get the rewards, and my parents were always making it clear that that was how my sisters and I should live our lives. From an early age, even when I was playing really well for my Sunday team, the Ridgeway Rovers, my dad would just say, "You played well today, boy, well done," and that was that. There was no ceremony or wave after wave of compliments. Even Alex Ferguson praised me more

CHILDHOOD DREAMS_

at United than my dad did back then!

Dad's attitude was helpful because from that early age I always wanted to do better. If I played poorly, mind you, it was the exact opposite; he would always tell me in great detail just how bad I was. Every shot that I missed, every cross that I should have gotten over, every pass that I misplaced—he would tell me exactly where I went wrong.

I guess it was up to me to remember the good games I had, and there were a few, I promise. I remember once we beat a team 21-0, which was some performance. Before you start to feel sorry for the opposition, that day was about us being very good rather than them being awful.

The Ridgeway Rovers were a great club. I was only seven when a new local team run by a guy called Stuart Underwood was set up. I went along for a trial, must have impressed, and suddenly I had my first club. Stuart was great and there was nothing amateur about how he ran the club. Yes, we had a lot of fun in the Rovers, but even at that young age, if I had a bad game, Stuart was always on hand to let me know. I had my dad in one ear and Stuart in another—talk about getting it from all angles!

Being a Ridgeway Rover made you feel special. They have gone on, from those days at Chase Park in London, to become a Sunday soccer phenomenon, and to be part of it was great. We would go on tours in Europe to places like Holland and Germany. That was so memorable, as us boys loved traveling and playing foreign opposition. It made us feel special, but above all we felt professional. That's what trips like that and a place like The Academy can do for young players.

As a boy, I was always looking for somewhere to kick a ball around. The park, a playground, my parents' yard, any open place and you would find me kicking, shooting, or practicing my skills. Again, it's what kids do, and I would love pretending that I was playing for Manchester United or curling in the winning goal for my country, leaving the distraught Brazilian keeper with no chance. Trips to Europe with Stuart and the Ridgeway Rovers brought

"MUM, I'M GOING TO BE THE CAPTAIN OF ENGLAND WHEN I GROW UP."

★★★★★ 02.05.75

those dreams a little bit closer.

Alongside Stuart with the Rovers was a man named Steve Kirby who helped out. Steve owned a business that made track suits and so we were all decked out with these cool new outfits as well as a uniform. We looked awesome. We even had sponsors' names across our shirts. We still had oranges at halftime, but the general feel of our little club was extremely professional.

We'd train twice a week. My dad was always encouraging me to play and train, but for the majority of the time he had to work and so it was Mum who would drive me on Tuesday and Thursday no matter what. People can take that sort of support

for granted, but if you have your family behind you then it makes life so much easier; it allows you to get on with playing and enjoying your passion, and that's exactly what I did.

From the age of nine, I would travel with the club in shirt, tie, and jacket. A lot of the boys and their parents weren't happy with that particular rule, but Stuart Underwood insisted—and I loved it. It was like we were professionals.

I grew up there feeling like I was already a pro and that was fantastic. You'd spend Saturday night watching *Match of the Day*, seeing the players who you adored turning up to games in their club suits and then the next morning you were doing the same.

For me it made our Sunday soccer a bit more authentic and even more memorable. I couldn't get enough of it.

As a kid, when you see the players do something on television or at a game, you immediately want to do the same. Children are very impressionable and will mimic what they see. Because of that, we players do have a responsibility to do the right thing. In the heat of a match, it's not always easy, but we must try to keep that in mind. When I was a boy I wanted nothing more than to have the same hair as Manchester United's Gordon Strachan!

I know, I know, it's an odd one, but that's what I wanted. Okay, so it wasn't the color that I was after, but when Gordon arrived at Old Trafford from Aberdeen, he had his hair cut in this spiky style, which I loved. I was forever copying it and running far too much gel through my own hair. I once went to Old Trafford and took a tube of hair gel and gave it to him. He must have thought I was a really strange boy.

My bedroom was a shrine to Manchester United. My bedspread was United, my wallpaper was United, I had flags on the walls and a huge poster of Bryan Robson above my bed. You'd think my family would have grown tired of my obsession, but it was the opposite. My whole family was brought up with soccer in their blood. Even my sisters shared a fondness for the game; in fact my youngest sister often came to watch me train and play.

It was my dad of course who turned me onto the game as a whole, but also onto United. He was a huge fan. Despite being from London, he had grown up with the Busby Babes and was hooked. Bobby Charlton, Denis Law, and of course George Best were later his heroes and he had passed that fanaticism to me. Charlton, Law, and Best had been replaced by Robson, Hughes, and Whiteside, but I could always get a feel for my dad's generation through the hundreds of old videos he kept.

Every day, every night, there I was on the sofa hogging the television set, watching a new or old game on the VCR. If I wasn't in the park or ruining

"MY DAD NEVER STOPPED TELLING ME THAT YOU DON'T GET ANYWHERE WITHOUT PUTTING IN HOURS AND HOURS OF WORK."

the yard with a ball, there would be soccer on television.

As you will have gathered I was a bit of a fan, and because of that I couldn't possibly tell you what I would be doing if I hadn't become a soccer player. I haven't got a clue! In my mind, there was never any other option. It was just assumed that I would be a professional and if I'm honest I never really concentrated on anything else.

In high school I *did* show an interest in a number of subjects. I took home economics (it was either that or double science!) but Gordon Ramsay needn't worry, I'm far from a good cook. I also liked music and even sang a solo in the school choir. My favorite subject, though, was art. I loved to draw cartoons. If I remember correctly, Donald Duck was my forte!

Soccer was always the passion, though, but after a while I began to draw cartoons that involved soccer and the guys in the Ridgeway Rovers. I should have continued, I could have started a new comic.

Of course, growing up brought other distractions. As a teenager there are plenty of diversions. Your friends, going out, girls, but to be honest I went on with my soccer. Back then I wasn't interested in anything else.

Another obsession of mine was skateboarding. All my friends would go over to the park and be on their skateboards having a brilliant time. I was banned from the ramps because my mum got tired of me coming home with all sorts of bumps and bruises. I loved my skateboard, though, and would find ways of sneaking out and doing it on the quiet. Sorry, Mum.

Back when I was a kid, there weren't nearly as many distractions. Kids now have all sorts of toys and things to do but in my day we had a far simpler way of life. We could spend literally the whole day in the park playing one game of soccer. The score may have ended up something like 37-35, but we loved it and dreaded the call from our mums to come in to have our dinner.

We had computers, but nothing like they are today. I remember the game *Daley Thompson's Decathlon*, which had you bashing the computer's keys like crazy. Never mind my skateboard, you could get a nasty injury playing that.

Saturday night would come around and my friends would turn up and ask if I was coming out. The answer was always no. I would stay in, get on the sofa, and watch soccer with my dad, in preparation for my own match the next morning. I'd tell them to go on without me—I was getting ready for the game.

"AS A KID, WHEN YOU SEE THE PLAYERS DO SOMETHING ON TELEVISION OR AT A GAME, YOU IMMEDIATELY WANT TO DO THE SAME."

2
BALL
CONTROL__

Okay, so good ball control isn't exactly a part of the game that we think will have the fans jumping from their seats and screaming your name. It's not going to have the journalists and commentators searching for the right words to describe your genius. It's not like that killer pass, or that fantastic shot from a distance, but without good ball control and without a good first touch those spectacular moments just aren't going to happen.

Having an assured first touch and being confident in your ball control allows a player to get on with concentrating on what he or she does next and does best. Players such as Zinedine Zidane and Ronaldinho entertain us all with their tricks that look so effortless, but those same tricks are down to good players' ability to control the ball without even thinking about it.

Wherever I have played, be it for Manchester United, Real Madrid, or England, I have looked to get the ball under control with a good, reliable first touch before getting on with the task of passing, crossing, or shooting.

Ball control for me is vital. When I was a kid it was probably the most important thing that was drilled into me by my dad. Even when I was as young as seven, he would kick the ball as high as he could and get me to control it with either foot. I used to hate doing it over and over again because I just wanted to shoot the ball at him, practice my long passes, and score goals, but he worked and worked on it with me and it's only later when you play in the Premiership or La Liga that you realize just how vital that first touch is. A good first touch gives you more time, and time on the soccer field is as valuable a commodity as you're likely to find.

Like every skill in soccer, you will get better and better at it with good practice. That's why I'm so grateful to my dad for instilling that work ethic in me, ensuring that basic ball control became a very strong part of my game.

With good practice, it becomes second nature. A ball can come at you at any part of your body, and at any pace; if you have practiced your ball control, you can manipulate that pass and have it immediately under your command. Work hard at it and it will eventually come naturally.

Having warmed up, it is a good idea to simply move around the field with the ball at your feet. This brings ball familiarity and that is priceless. Become comfortable with that ball. The more comfortable you are, the less you have to think about controlling it, and the more you can think about what you are going to do with it next.

Move with the ball, change your pace, change the angle, try a trick, move the ball with the outside of the foot and the inside of the foot. Fake to go one way and move the ball the other. Keep working your mind as well as your feet and get a real feel for having the ball under your control.

Look at Zidane. It has been a pleasure watching him at Madrid as he has the ability to run at players, his head always up, always looking for his next pass or his next dribble and he can do that knowing full well that the ball is more than comfortable at his feet.

When controlling the ball, remain relaxed. If you tense the body, that touch will be forced and rigid. Remain relaxed and the touch will be smooth, confident, and far more effective.

At any level of soccer, you can expect to be closed down very quickly, so if you can be confident when receiving a pass, you already have one over that defender who is intent on getting the better of you.

Your first touch is arguably the most important aspect of playing soccer. As I say, it doesn't win you as many cheers but it is the perfect springboard for those other, perhaps more showy, parts of the game. If you have a good first touch, then you give yourself far more time. With time on the ball (and the great players in the world all seem to have that sense of time) you have the ability to size up your different options. A good first touch will enable you to think about the alternatives that exist; it will help you make the right decisions and hopefully cause your opponents the maximum of damage.

If your first touch is off, the chances are the defender will cut in and steal the ball from you, so it is vital you are comfortable with bringing the ball under control as quickly as you can.

A common fault for many young players is trying to kill the ball dead with their first touch. If you kill it dead like that and it sticks under your feet, you then have to adjust your body and step back before trying to regain your momentum. That allows the defender to gather his or her senses, take up the best position, and even steal the ball.

With their first touch a good player will get the ball out of their feet and be ready to go. Don't be frightened to make that first touch a heavy one, one that takes the ball away from you, allowing you to move onto it and be positive. It's all about gaining knowledge about your own personal surroundings, having the confidence to manipulate the ball while always keeping it under control.

"WHEN I WAS A KID IT WAS PROBABLY THE MOST IMPORTANT THING THAT WAS DRILLED INTO ME BY MY DAD."

FIRST TOUCH_

INSIDE OF FOOT

Always be on your toes, expecting the ball and therefore ready and confident to receive it.

Let your teammates know where and when you want the ball with good, clear verbal instructions.

When receiving the ball, keep your head steady and up so you know exactly what is going on around you.

Try to receive it with the body half turned (sideways to the ball) while using your arms for both balance and protection.

With your first touch, use the inside of the foot to take the ball away from your body and therefore also away from the defender. Make sure that first touch is just right so it gets out from under your feet and into space but not too far so that you have to go chasing it.

Get onto the ball as quickly as possible, keeping your head up so that you are ready for your next move, be it a pass, a cross, or a shot.

INSIDE OF FOOT ACROSS YOUR BODY

As well as simply using the inside of the foot to take the ball away from you, also use it to carry the ball across your body. This first touch unsettles defenders. By taking the ball from right to left and left to right you again give yourself the chance to get the ball from out of your feet and away from the defender. As before, always be willing to get onto that ball as quickly as possible.

Of course, you are not always going to receive the perfect ball, and it won't always be possible to simply control it with the inside of your foot. Because of that, you need to be comfortable and at ease with controlling the ball with other parts of your foot and your body.

OUTSIDE OF FOOT

The outside of the foot can be a clever method of controlling the ball but also very effective. If a pass is underhit, you will find it easier sometimes to simply use this part of the foot to get the ball under control, remembering the same principle as before. Make sure that first touch takes the ball away from your feet and away from the defender. As ever, be prepared to get onto the ball as soon as you have touched it away.

"YOUR FIRST TOUCH IS ARGUABLY THE MOST IMPORTANT ASPECT OF PLAYING SOCCER."

THIGH

The thigh, like the chest, is another crucial part of the body when it comes to getting the ball under control quickly and easily.

As the ball comes toward you, offer the surface of the thigh.

On impact, relax the thigh to cushion the ball, allowing it to drop at your feet before moving the ball confidently away from your body and into space for your next pass, cross, or shot.

CHEST

Receiving a long pass while at the same time surrounded by defenders is never going to be easy. But if you are aware that you can use more than simply your foot to control the ball, you are already at an advantage. The chest is very useful when controlling a pass, especially when that pass is hit through the air.

Move your body quickly into position so that you are in line with the flight of the ball.

In preparation, make sure the body is relaxed before receiving the ball.

As the ball comes toward you, bend the knees and arch the lower back to absorb the impact.

As the ball bounces off the chest, be prepared to use another part of the body (e.g. the thigh or the inside of the foot) to keep the ball under control.

Often, you will have to receive a long ball that comes out of the sky and therefore bounces before it reaches you. Here, you must be comfortable and confident that your first touch will kill that bounce and allow you to have the ball under your control as soon as possible. That defender is again going to be on you like a flash, so a good first touch will once more lessen his or her threat.

However many defenders are around you, remain calm, relax the body, and let the surface of the body part you are using act as a sponge to absorb the impact of the ball.

CONTROLLING A BOUNCING BALL

HEAD

Like the chest and the inside of the foot, the head is very useful when it comes to controlling a bouncing ball.

With the ball bouncing at head height, relax the body and the neck to cushion the impact of the ball on contact.

As before, be prepared to use a secondary part of the body to control the ball as it drops to the feet.

As ever, use that second touch to take the ball away from the body and into space.

INSIDE OF FOOT

As the ball bounces in front of you, keep your eye on it at all times while at the same time making sure that you are in control of your body.

Keep your knee above the bouncing ball and ensure that first touch is a strong and confident one.

Take the ball with the inside of the foot, making sure you place the ball exactly where you want it, be that away from your body or across it. Either way, take the ball away from your feet and from the defenders into the nearby space.

CHEST

The ball can bounce too high to get that knee over it and bring it under control using the foot, and that's when the chest can once again be very useful.

As the ball is in the air, use the chest to cushion it before taking it away from your body and the defender by using either the inside or the outside of the foot.

If need be, you should be more than prepared to take that ball with your weaker foot. It may seem unnatural, but the more you work at it, the more normal it will become.

Nearly three years ago I was sitting in my house in Madrid with my old friend and manager Terry Byrne. We were chatting about what I'd like to do once the soccer season finished and I said I would like to build soccer schools. It seems a weird thing to want to do, but Terry could see I was deadly serious. I wanted to build schools in a way that had never been done before.

I wanted to get the best coaches, the best personnel, and the best facilities and give the kids the best time possible. "You want to build the soccer equivalent of Charlie's Chocolate Factory," laughed Terry.

So, we had the idea, but the next step was to make it a reality. I had a clear image in my mind of what I wanted, so we could get the ball rolling and use our contacts within the game to hire the right people and make sure that side of things was as perfect as could be. We got good coaches and the right medical staff involved and we went from there.

With the help of Simon Fuller, 19 Entertainment, and our partners at Anschutz Entertainment Group, we

THE ACADEMY: CONCEPT_

found the spot we liked near the old Millennium Dome and approached the Greenwich Council for planning permission. What they liked about our proposal was that we promised that 10,000 school kids a year would come to The Academy, free of charge, and 2,000 of them would attend from local schools. We were granted permission and from there everything started to take shape.

The builders moved in and got to work on what today is an awe-inspiring place. I remember when I first went along to have a look once it was finished. I was with Terry again (pictured opposite with Eric Harrison and my mum), who had worked so hard on the project, and the place took my breath away. Here I was in my first Academy. From a conversation in Madrid, a building had been built and the project was soon to be up and running. It was a magic moment.

I was lucky that I had people around me who understood my vision and helped me make it real. Because of their hard work we have The David Beckham Academies in London and Los Angeles, and in 2007 we hope to have one opened in Asia.

My Academy is the only facility in all of Europe that has two full-sized soccer fields under one roof. The classrooms are wonderful, the technology is there, the staff are there, the medical backup is

"I WANTED TO BUILD SCHOOLS — AND TERRY [BYRNE] COULD SEE I WAS DEADLY SERIOUS."

there. On top of that there is a fabulous kitchen. I'm told by the kids that the lasagne is fantastic. The main goal is for the kids to have a fun experience through soccer.

The long-term vision for the place is to maintain the highest standards of soccer coaching for kids. I want this place to produce some children who can go all the way and have careers as professional soccer players, but as I said, that's not the main aim of my Academy.

That has surprised a few people who obviously think that because I have made a career out of playing soccer then I should automatically want to create an Academy that helps others do the same, but that's not the case. It's not just about great players, kids who can play the game and who will excel at soccer. It's about a place where kids can come and learn, where they can be safe and where they can have fun.

As I say, when I went to Bobby Charlton's school I got such delight from meeting my heroes and getting so close up to the professional game in general. At The Academy I have plenty of the original cleats and shirts that I have worn over the years in some of my biggest games, on display for all to see. I hope the wow factor that we are trying to achieve happens as soon as the kids come through the doors.

"I HOPE THE WOW FACTOR THAT WE ARE TRYING TO ACHIEVE HAPPENS AS SOON AS THE KIDS COME THROUGH THE DOORS."

We know, however, that we can't live off how good the place looks. Kids get bored—any parent will tell you that—and even if they are at Wembley Stadium but are having a dull time they are going to let you know about it. They might as well just be in the local park. You have to deliver something that is both relevant and exciting.

The soccer camps and the day visits are unique. The whole thing has to live up to the venue with a unique product. We are aiming at longevity for The Academy and that means getting things right and making it as fun and effective as possible.

Many professional clubs and their associated academies organize community programs taking mixed-ability kids, running camps, after-school clubs, and the like—in fact, all the things we are doing—but we feel we have the advantage. We have the facility, but also an approach that concentrates on the ethics of the game and promotes the right behavior. It's alright not to be the best player around; it's okay not to be able to play at a high level. You can want to get better—that's more than encouraged—but you must respect that all your teammates and opponents are different and have a right to be treated fairly.

Out of thirty kids, the majority will be average, but then you have small pockets of kids who aren't very strong and small pockets of kids who are very talented. We have to work with all of them in equal measure.

3
MAKING SPACE_

Making space is a huge part of my game. I have spent much of my career wide on the right and it has been vital that I give my teammates an option to pass to me. That means getting myself in good space to receive a pass. Having received that pass, I need a yard of space so I can cross that ball into the box or play a ball up to the forwards. I'm not the sort of player who runs at defenders and beats them with a dribble. I have to have that good first touch to take the ball a yard away from me, and then make space before unleashing what hopefully will be the killer cross or pass.

The term "making space" may seem a bit dull. Don't worry, I was the same when I was growing up. As kids we just want to get the ball and score goals. I know I did. The temptation sometimes, though, is to all run toward the ball without thinking. We hunt it down without purpose and without shape. Instead of running toward the ball we should think about running away from it and getting into space so you can receive the ball and cause problems.

I have had to learn this skill as I have progressed as a player. Having played for Manchester United and Real Madrid, it is something I have had to get used to and master. Both clubs value possession. Both have had great players who are always going to see a lot of the ball, and therefore it is vital that you are able to create and exploit space. I need to be available to receive a pass from Zidane and then make myself a yard so I can make my own pass to Raul or Ronaldo.

I come up against some of the best defenders in the world, so I have to work hard on ways to trick them, to give myself the upper hand and therefore help my team. Making space is all about working on your ball control, using your brains and coming up with new ways to deceive the defender.

The better your ball control the less space you will need, so remember to work on that first touch. That will ensure that the ball is under your command as quickly as possible, leaving you to concentrate on your next move. It has been said that soccer should be a simple game, and that's right. If you can master doing the simple things with ease but at a good pace, you are on your way to becoming a top player.

Practice your first touch, become comfortable with the ball at your feet, and then you can work on creating for yourself those most valued of things on a soccer field, time and space. I recommend practicing with your friends. Get yourself into small games. If there are only three or four of you, play two on one or two on two. Create a small field, working on receiving the ball in a condensed space and making time for yourself to return that pass. Keep the movement lively and your touch sharp.

Work on receiving and passing the ball before exploiting the space behind the defense.

With a defender behind you, move toward the player with the ball.

Receive their pass and give it straight back with the inside of your foot.

Having returned the pass, turn quickly and explode into the space behind the defender. You are then available to receive the next pass.

When receiving the pass, make sure your first touch is a good one, look to pass the ball back, and then burst into space. Without the ball, you can drag defenders around by faking to go one way before exploiting the space they have left.

As I say, we also need to look at how we use space when we have the ball. A trick or a fake can buy you the time you require but again this stems from practicing your ball control and feeling comfortable on the ball. Be confident.

There are plenty of ways we can make space. Here I fake to go one way and buy myself some space before exploding in the opposite direction.

One minute I am in my shrine of a bedroom, idolizing the players, the history, everything about the place; the next minute I'm signing forms and I'm actually a Manchester United player. Being from London and obviously playing all my soccer down in the southeast, I often thought I would get overlooked by my childhood heroes.

The closest I had gotten to soccer and the city I so wished to play in were my visits to Bobby Charlton's Soccer School in Manchester. I was ten when I first went to Bobby's school and couldn't believe my luck. I had heard about it from an episode of *Blue Peter* and hassled my parents until they had to let me go. I mean, I had seen all those videos of the great Bobby Charlton and now here was a chance to play and learn with him, and all of this would happen in Manchester. It was like all my Christmases had come at once.

The school was great. I must say I was only ten when I first went up there and while I loved the soccer I felt a bit homesick, what with being away the whole week. I had been suffering with a bit of a toothache as well so I was very keen to go back the following year and give it another go.

I was much more confident the second time around and started to impress. Each group had a skills competition through the week, which tested you on shooting, long passing, short passing, ball juggling, and dribbling. The winner from each week was invited to Old Trafford for the grand final the following December and yours truly managed to come out on top. I was off to Old Trafford. Old Trafford! For a boy whose bedroom was decked out in all things red, this was going to be incredible.

We had to do more skills tests out on the field with 40,000 fans packed into the stands. United was playing the Spurs that day and being from London, I got a good reception from both sets of fans when it was announced that I had won. It was Bobby himself who presented me with a trophy and the trip of a lifetime to Barcelona, where I would visit the famous Nou Camp and meet some of the players.

Back then Terry Venables was the Spanish giants' manager, Gary Lineker was their goal scorer, but it was Mark Hughes, one of my heroes from his time at United and a future teammate, who excited me the most. It was a fabulous trip, one in which I was able to get my first taste of Spanish soccer when I trained

LIVING THE DREAM_

with the Barcelona youth team at the stadium.

As I got older and started drawing attention from scouts it was London clubs that were initially interested, but my heart belonged to United, and so when a man called Malcolm Fidgeon called saying he was a scout from Old Trafford and they would like to give me a tryout, it was like Christmas and FA Cup Final day all rolled into one.

Suddenly the Ridgeway Rovers shirt and tie is replaced with a Manchester United blazer and all your dreams have come true. All that hard work has paid off, but I knew that this was only the beginning and that this was where the real hard work had to begin.

With Alex Ferguson around, a kid at United knew not to get ahead of himself. It would be easy to get a bit cocky and feel a bit more superior to others. But again, I was lucky. I had so many people around me who were so good for me and who kept me grounded, both in and out of the club. At home, of course, I had my mum and dad, while inside Old Trafford there was not only the manager but also Eric Harrison, who looked after the youth team. With Eric around, you couldn't get away with anything.

That's why I wanted Eric involved at my Academy. He has drawn up a coaching manual that all our coaches work from. We call it the Bible because to

me there is no one more qualified than Eric to pass on his experience in the game, both to kids and to the men and women who teach them.

I wanted Eric involved because he has been such a huge part of my life and my career, both as a coach and a father figure. Without Eric, I honestly think that many of the young lads at United would not be in the fantastic position we are today. Gary and Phil Neville, Paul Scholes, and me, to name but a few, owe him a lot. I think it's great that I can turn to someone like Eric, a man and a coach who has helped me so much with my soccer, for further advice for those kids who come to my Academy.

Thanks to Eric and the staff at United, I enjoyed the most incredible times with the club I idolized from afar as a boy. The highs in my career astound me and I would in no way ever take them for granted. People are always asking me to name *the* highlight in my career, but it's not that easy. There have been so many, and I'm not just talking about the obvious moments like winning domestic and European trophies, scoring the free kick that took England to the World Cup in 2002, or captaining my country's team.

I also look back on my career so far and cherish the less glamorous moments, the moments that are special to me personally, away from the glare and the spotlight. The day I signed with United, for instance, winning the Milk Cup with United's youth team, captaining that team, my debut for the senior team at Brighton in the Coca-Cola Cup (as it was known back then), my league debut against Leeds, my Champions League debut against Galatasaray, a game in which I also scored my first-ever goal for the club. There I was at Old Trafford playing against European opposition: I hit the ball and it's in the back of the net in front of the famous old Stretford End. I turn to celebrate and there's Eric Cantona, the first on hand to congratulate his grinning teammate. Those moments are all so special to me and I will never forget them.

Of course, I will also always cherish winning the six Premiership crowns with United, the FA Cup, and the Treble in 1999. I have had so many special moments right up to the present day, where I find myself playing for Real Madrid and living with my family in Spain. I'm proud to have had the privilege of playing

"I HAD SO MANY PEOPLE AROUND ME WHO WERE SO GOOD FOR ME AND WHO KEPT ME GROUNDED."

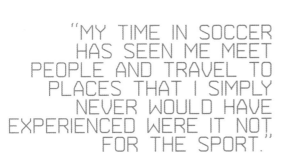

"MY TIME IN SOCCER HAS SEEN ME MEET PEOPLE AND TRAVEL TO PLACES THAT I SIMPLY NEVER WOULD HAVE EXPERIENCED WERE IT NOT FOR THE SPORT."

with two of the greatest clubs in the world, Manchester United and Real Madrid. Not bad for a boy who grew up playing on Hackney Marshes.

I would be lying though if I said that my career has only been about incredible highs. Everyone has to face lows in their life and in their work and I certainly have. When you're in the public eye, I think those lows are even bigger than when you are not. The important thing again is to have the right people around you. Those people have been on hand to make sure I didn't get too big-headed when things began to go so well, but they have also been there to help when things have gone wrong.

I have a great family, great parents, my sisters, friends; they have all helped, and now my own children and my wife are always on hand to lift the gloom if I feel I haven't played as well as I know I can. Without them the pressures of the job would be that much harder to handle. All players suffer losses

of form, but it's how you deal with that blip that is crucial. The hard times can actually make you a stronger person and a better player. You have to learn and keep learning, not only when you are a youngster making your way in the game but as a seasoned pro. The day you feel you can stop learning is probably the day you should hang up the cleats and say good-bye to the game.

Speaking of learning, I have had so many great coaches in my time in soccer and hope to bring a bit of each to The Academy. I'm not only talking about the obvious guys such as Alex Ferguson or Sven-Goran Eriksson. They have been huge influences, but I owe a lot to the guys behind the scenes, the guys who have coached me, from a young age, day in and day out.

I started at United with Nobby Stiles. Nobby was great. He was a legend at the club and while being very

"THE HIGHS IN MY CAREER ASTOUND ME AND I WOULD IN NO WAY EVER TAKE THEM FOR GRANTED."

tough, he was an amazing character and you couldn't help but be influenced by his infectious zest for life, for United, and for soccer. I then had Bryan "Pop" Robson, Eric Harrison, Brian Kidd, and the new England boss, Steve McClaren. All of them were great coaches and their input to my game has been invaluable. Even the best players need great teachers along the way and these guys are the men I owe so much to.

I was pleased to hear that Steve McClaren had got the England job. As I have said, I have worked with a lot of coaches, very good coaches at that, and Steve is right up there with the best. I obviously got to know Steve well from my time with him at Old Trafford but the England players, too, have grown to know and respect Steve from his role as Eriksson's number two. Ask any of the players in the England set-up and they will tell you that he is a good coach. He has done brilliant things at Middlesbrough and more than deserves his chance.

When he joined United in 1999 as a replacement for Brian Kidd, Steve didn't disrupt what was already there. Instead he worked with what he had and helped it to improve. We of course went on to win the treble in his first few months at the club, so he was clearly doing something right.

Because of all the people who have helped me on my journey and because of what I have managed to achieve, I feel very honored. Through soccer, I have been able to build a wonderful life and I can fall back on so many incredible memories. Through my Academy I feel I can now give something back to the game and to kids. Children are our future, and for them to have somewhere to come, to be safe, and to learn about more than simply playing the game is such a joy and that's what we are trying to achieve.

My time in soccer has seen me meet people and travel to places that I simply never would have experienced were it not for the sport. I have traveled the world, and again I could never take that privilege for granted. We as players are lucky but the public probably doesn't realize that more often than not, we don't get to see as much of a place as some of us would like.

Too often, we are in hotels, training camps, buses, and stadiums where it's difficult to appreciate a country or a city. Sometimes you'll be playing somewhere lovely and you'll wish you could stay longer to get a feel for the place. Having said that, and I'm naming no names, there are times when you just want to get your game done, get straight out of there, and get home to the family. It all depends where you are.

I've now been traveling the world and playing the game I grew up with in the park for over fourteen years. Today when I run out at Madrid or for my country I still get the same buzz I did on that cold night in Brighton back in 1992 when I made my debut. In fact I probably enjoy it more. That night on the south coast, I was sitting on the bench watching my teammates, who only months before had been my heroes, and I was so nervous. I was desperate to get on, but if I did would I make a mistake, was I going to make the grade?

With twenty minutes to go, the manager turned to me: "Get changed, son, you're going on." I was so excited I bounced up off my seat and *crack*: I hit my head on the roof of the dugout. Not the best of starts, although it would be front-page news if that sort of thing happened today.

DB7

4

TURNING_

Like basic ball control and creating space, an ability to turn with the ball is very important. Like those other disciplines, it may not be all that flashy, but when done correctly it not only switches your team's play but also creates the chance to get in the net, leading to a cross, shot, and hopefully a goal.

A turn can open up a defense. You can fake to go one way but with one quick turn you can be away and a defense is left flat-footed and exposed. It's massive and a very important part of an attacking player's weapons. As ever, the more we practice our turns, the more comfortable we become and the more familiar we are with the ball. The key, though, to a good turn is that ever-important first touch.

You control a ball, you make space by turning, and you're off with the ball. No one can stop you!

Practice turning with your friends. All you need is a ball and some open space.

With cones, mark out lanes for you and a partner to run along with the ball.

Take the ball to the end of the line, turn, and come back for your partner to take over. The ball must be moving all the time and it's vital you vary the method of turning. The turn can be a fake; the first touch can be outside of the foot, the inside, or the sole depending on the turn. That first touch must make the ball move, must be hard enough to take the ball away from your feet, and then the second touch is more controlled. Basic technique requires the second touch to be with the nearest part of the nearest foot irrespective of the turn.

The Gianfranco Zolas of this world are great at a quick turn, even in the smallest of spaces. Their first touch would be so good and the acceleration over six feet so explosive that they would be away from the defenders. We can all do these turns, but with practice we can begin to excel at them at pace and when under pressure from defenders.

Here I want to look at how best to turn with the ball when you have your back to the goal. As an attacker receiving that ball with no apparent danger, a defender will hate you if you possess the ability to

"THE GIANFRANCO ZOLAS OF THIS WORLD ARE GREAT AT A QUICK TURN, EVEN IN THE SMALLEST OF SPACES."

beat them with a turn and get a cross or a shot away. Practice and practice and then, even if you are facing away from the goal, you still represent a huge danger.

When receiving the ball, turn sideways, always looking over the shoulder to check on the defender's movements and that a turn is okay.

Let the ball move across the body.

With the inside of the foot furthest away from the pass, cushion the ball into space.

Accelerate away into the space. Remember, it is vital that you move into the turn at pace. This will take you away from the defender.

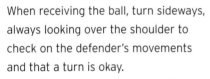

_TURNING USING THE INSIDE OF THE FOOT

"THE BETTER YOUR BALL CONTROL, THE LESS SPACE YOU WILL NEED."

Make your first touch a good one, taking the ball from out of your feet.

Disguise your movement by taking a step beyond the ball before taking the ball the other way with the outside of the opposite foot.

Get onto the ball as quick as you can, ready for your next move (i.e., a cross, shot, or a pass).

OUTSIDE HOOK_

The step over is a nice trick. It is simple in as much as you don't actually have to touch the ball, but when done correctly it can trick the best defender and give you that vital bit of space.

Your first touch should be confident, but make sure you stop the ball, keeping it at your feet.

Move your body and foot over the ball as if about to speed off in one direction.

Take a second touch, moving the ball quickly away with the outside of the foot in the opposite direction.

Get onto the ball quickly, ready for your next move.

STEP OVER_

Again, this is a way of disguising your actions and tricking a defender into giving you the space you require.

Make sure your first touch takes the ball from out of your feet.

Fake to kick the ball, but instead take a second touch with the inside of the foot, moving the ball across your body.

The third touch is with the outside of the opposite foot and takes the ball away, ready for your next move.

_INSIDE HO S

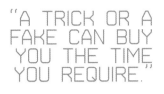

"A TRICK OR A
FAKE CAN BUY
YOU THE TIME
YOU REQUIRE."

With your first touch, take the ball to the side.

Using the foot furthest away from the defender, stop the ball with the sole of the foot before dragging it back through the legs so you're facing the way you came.

As you turn, use the outside of the opposite foot to take the ball into the available space.

Get onto the ball quickly, ready for your next move.

_STOP TURN

This is one of my favorites, made famous by the legendary Dutch star of the 1960s and '70s, Johan Cruyff. I like to use this a lot and if it comes off at pace it looks great, especially as it's all about disguise.

- With your first touch, take the ball to the side.
- Plant your non-striking foot firmly beyond the ball.
- Shape to either cross or shoot the ball.
- With your second touch use the inside of the foot to play the ball in the opposite direction.
- Get onto the ball quickly, ready for your next move.

With all these techniques it is important that you not only practice them again and again (don't be scared of messing up) but that you are aware of the different parts of the foot that you can use.

Work on your ball control and continue to use the inside and outside of both feet.

_CRUYFF TURN

This is useful when you have a defender right behind you.

When receiving the ball, look over your shoulder so you are aware of the defender's movements.

Drag the ball away, with the inside of your foot away from the defender.

Feel free to take another touch if you feel you need to get away from the defender.

Accelerate into space at the side of the defender.

DRAG-BACK WITH THE INSIDE OF THE FOOT_

Again, this is a way of disguising your actions and tricking a defender into giving you the space you require.

Make sure your first touch takes the ball from out of your feet.

Fake to kick the ball, but instead take a second touch with the inside of the foot, moving the ball across your body.

The third touch is with the outside of the opposite foot and takes the ball away, ready for your next move.

_INSIDE HOOK

The step over is a nice trick. It is simple in as much as you don't actually have to touch the ball, but when done correctly it can trick the best defender and give you that vital bit of space.

Your first touch should be confident, but make sure you stop the ball, keeping it at your feet.

Move your body and foot over the ball as if about to speed off in one direction.

Take a second touch, moving the ball quickly away with the outside of the foot in the opposite direction.

Get onto the ball quickly, ready for your next move.

STEP OVER_

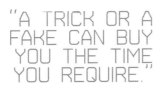

"A TRICK OR A
FAKE CAN BUY
YOU THE TIME
YOU REQUIRE."

With your first touch, take the ball to the side.

Using the foot furthest away from the defender, stop the ball with the sole of the foot before dragging it back through the legs so you're facing the way you came.

As you turn, use the outside of the opposite foot to take the ball into the available space.

Get onto the ball quickly, ready for your next move.

_STOP TURN

This is one of my favorites, made famous by the legendary Dutch star of the 1960s and '70s, Johan Cruyff. I like to use this a lot and if it comes off at pace it looks great, especially as it's all about disguise.

- With your first touch, take the ball to the side.
- Plant your non-striking foot firmly beyond the ball.
- Shape to either cross or shoot the ball.
- With your second touch use the inside of the foot to play the ball in the opposite direction.
- Get onto the ball quickly, ready for your next move.

With all these techniques it is important that you not only practice them again and again (don't be scared of messing up) but that you are aware of the different parts of the foot that you can use.

Work on your ball control and continue to use the inside and outside of both feet.

_CRUYFF TURN

This is useful when you have a defender right behind you.

When receiving the ball, look over your shoulder so you are aware of the defender's movements.

Drag the ball away, with the inside of your foot away from the defender.

Feel free to take another touch if you feel you need to get away from the defender.

Accelerate into space at the side of the defender.

DRAG-BACK WITH THE INSIDE OF THE FOOT_

"REMEMBER, IT IS VITAL THAT YOU MOVE INTO THE TURN AT PACE."

This one is very effective when done at pace.

If the ball toward you is very quick and along the ground, let it roll off the outside of the foot into the space at the side of the defender.

Accelerate after the ball, leaving that poor defender in your wake.

_LETTING THE BALL ROLL OFF THE OUTSIDE OF THE FOOT

Again, with your back to the goal, this is a way of beating your marker.

Fake to take the ball across your body with the inside of your foot.

Instead take a soft touch, almost stopping the ball.

Use the outside of the foot to take the ball in the opposite direction.

Accelerate into the space you've so cleverly created.

When receiving the ball with your back to the goal, make sure you are aware of your teammates' positions but, even more importantly, be aware of the defenders'.

Turn quickly; it is the pace of your movements that will outfox the defender.

Always accelerate away from the turn.

Another way of practicing these different techniques is to get with your friends into a smallish square space. Each of you should have the ball and be moving around that space, every now and then trying a different turn using the inside, the outside, and the sole of the foot.

Always keep your head up so as not to collide with your friends.

Keep those knees bent for balance and, as ever, accelerate out of the turn, remaining in control of the ball.

DOUBLE TOUCH

It's one thing knowing exactly what kind of academy you want to set up, but it's another trying to get the right people behind the scenes who can help make that vision a reality. I have been very lucky in that I have, through my time in the game, made great contacts. I have worked with some of the best coaches around and because of that I can draw on their experience to make my Academy as strong as I always hoped it would be.

The staff are all so vital. They are hand-picked, as we want each person who works here to fit in and do the right thing. All the staff are brilliant with kids and that is paramount.

As I mentioned before, when I was a kid at United, I was lucky to come across Eric Harrison (pictured above), who looked after the youth team and was responsible for nurturing not only me but also the likes of Gary and Phil Neville, Ryan Giggs, Paul Scholes, and Nicky Butt; all of them now international players.

Eric has been good enough to help draw up a coaching manual for The Academy, and it's great to have him involved. Locating The Academy in London means I've come full circle in one way, but working once more with Eric takes me back to the beginning of my professional career with Manchester United, and I know other kids will benefit, as I did, from his wisdom.

He knows every coach, he knows about every possible coaching situation, and, above all, he knows what is best for kids, and you can't buy that. I can bring my experience in the game to the place but I'm no qualified coach. I have said I'm not interested in becoming a manager, but by choosing the right people and by passing on what knowledge I have, The Academy can be a massive success.

Alongside Eric is the director of coaching, Ted Dale (pictured opposite). Ted was Terry Byrne's first appointment. Terry knew all about Ted's expertise, and it is Ted who has a major say in the how the kids are coached, it is he who helps recruit The Academy's coaches, and it is he who writes the coaching programs. The combination of Eric and Ted ensures that the kids get the best in coaching know-how.

Terry became aware of Ted's work at Chelsea, having seen him bring on young talent such as John Terry at Stamford Bridge. Ted is a great character and a vital part of The London Academy set-up.

Of course, there are many other people at The Academy whose hard work and incredible enthusiasm make it such a wonderful place. There are 30 or so staff, including medical staff, dedicated coaches, and administrative staff. With their input each kid can take the absolute maximum from their

THE ACADEMY: STAFF AND SET-UP_

days, week, or evening at The Academy.

We see it like this: Kids should leave us with an increased sense of self-esteem. If you have low self-esteem when you walk in, we want to help change that. Through coaching and learning, kids can feel better about themselves, and that is a very exciting ambition for everyone involved.

We also have an obligation to turn kids on to sports. Getting picked last for a team conjures up images of a sad young child left feeling bad about themselves. Many youngsters won't play soccer because they won't get into a team of eleven, or perhaps they're just scared they won't. The very thought puts them off.

What we should be saying is, that's alright. The people at The Academy know it's okay to not be very good, and that those who are on the team can help. There is a place for you within a team. Sports shouldn't threaten a child's personality and we want to get that across. There should be no blame, no condemning. The Academy is non-judgmental from the time they come in to the time they leave.

When they leave, we want them to take that ethos with them. It's one thing coming here and loving it, but we want them to take that excitement with them and continue to enjoy playing and learning about the game. That means our Academy has to be relevant and real to their everyday lives. Sure, give them a great day at this wonderful place, but make sure they take something away with them, something they can use in the long term.

Soccer can bring so much happiness to kids: It can change a person's way of feeling, it lifts moods, and it brings people together. That's what we hope to achieve, and that's why we have set up The Academy in this way.

It's about much more than going out onto the field and playing. It's about learning about the game, learning about respect, learning about healthy eating, learning about injuries and how your body works.

If all you want to do is work with kids who show incredible talent and potential, kids who have all the ability, then you're no good here. This Academy is about bringing kids together, teaching unity, as well as learning how to treat your elders and your coaches with the right level of respect.

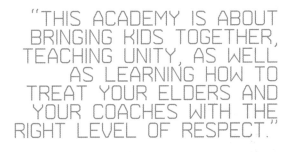

"THIS ACADEMY IS ABOUT BRINGING KIDS TOGETHER, TEACHING UNITY, AS WELL AS LEARNING HOW TO TREAT YOUR ELDERS AND YOUR COACHES WITH THE RIGHT LEVEL OF RESPECT."

5

PASSING_

f you know my game, you know I love to pass the ball. For me, there's nothing like seeing a ball you've played sail through the air, homing in on the exact target you were aiming for, before sending a teammate on his way. As a youngster I would get criticized by some coaches for playing what they called a "Hollywood pass." To some, that long ball is for show. Well, maybe it is a bit, but once perfected, there is no doubt it is a pass that can open up the most organized of defenses.

As a kid I used to love to watch Glenn Hoddle. I know, he wasn't a Manchester United player, but I forgave him for that due to his exceptional passing ability. I wanted to be able to pass like him and would once more practice like mad to get it right. Out in the park I'd put down cones and then from 30 or 40 yards would try again and again to hit them.

To me, passing is what the game is all about. It's a team game, after all, and the vast majority of what we do out on the field will involve passing the ball to our teammates, so it is vital that we are confident and able to make good and accurate passes. Losing possession means giving your opponents the chance to attack and maybe score against you. Get your passing right and your team will reap the rewards.

It isn't only our long passing, though, that we have to work on. Those "Hollywood passes" are all very well and good, but the vast majority of the passing we will be carrying out in a game will be short, swift movements that ensure our team maintains possession. These can be just as vital to the team as the defense-splitting "killer" pass and need just as much practice.

Everyone associates me with long passing, but having now played in Spain I have realized how important the art of a good short pass can be. They like to play it short at Real Madrid. I have been able to play that short pass throughout my career but have never had to do so regularly, and that means working harder on my game.

It is important to know where and when to take risks. The most memorable passes will occur in the attacking third of the field, but the majority will take place deeper and will be risk-free. Some players excel at the less-risky pass and that is vital, as the team's momentum is sustained and possession is rarely lost.

The problem with learning to pass the ball well is that many of us, professionals included, would rather keep hold of that ball, dribble around defenders, and perhaps hog all the limelight. That is normal, but it is vital that we learn that by playing as a team we get far greater results.

Think about it. What is the quickest thing on a soccer field? You? Thierry Henry? Wrong, the fastest thing on that field is the ball and by playing the ball to a target, you will get it there far quicker than running it there.

Make the ball do the running, move it around the field between you and your teammates and you'll realize just how satisfying passing can become.

It is important that you learn to make the right decisions—when to play that long "killer" pass and when to play a simpler ball that keeps possession for your team.

The inside of the foot is the most reliable surface to make a pass and will be your most useful tool when passing.

When receiving the ball, make sure you remember what we were doing with our ball control. The first touch should be a good one, taking the ball out of your feet. Look up so you know exactly where you want to place the ball. Remember, your target may well be moving.

The non-striking foot should be pointing in the direction in which you wish to play the ball and far enough to the side of the ball so as to not impede the striking foot.

Keep your eyes on the ball and your head steady as you strike the pass.

Keep your knee over the ball as you make contact to ensure you're fully in control.

Strike the middle of the ball with the inside of the foot and hold that position as you follow through.

Make sure that you have the right weight on your pass.

Never admire your pass. Always be moving into space and therefore willing to regain possession.

TWO-TOUCH WITH THE INSIDE OF THE FOOT_

"ONCE PERFECTED,
THERE IS NO DOUBT
IT IS A PASS THAT
CAN OPEN UP THE
MOST ORGANIZED
OF DEFENSES."

In any game, there are going to be times when you have to improvise, and by being able to use the outside of the foot to find a teammate you are increasing your options while also making a quicker, smarter pass. Using the outside of the foot, you can also generate swerve on the ball, allowing for a trickier ball.

With your first touch, take the ball across the body.

Use the outside of the foot, making sure the ankle is locked to ensure the pass is not underhit.

Again, be on the move as soon as you make the pass, giving your teammate an option and creating further space.

TWO-TOUCH WITH THE OUTSIDE OF THE FOOT

You won't always have time to take that first touch, so it is vital you are comfortable to pass the ball the first time.

- Keep your eye on the ball.
- Get your knee over the ball.
- Strike the ball in the middle.
- Place the non-kicking foot alongside the ball facing in the direction you want the ball to go.
- If the ball you are receiving is underhit, use more back lift, taking the striking foot back to generate pace.
- If it is overhit, cushion the ball with less back lift to keep control of your pass.
- Use the inside of the foot, locking the ankle, and hold that position as the foot follows through.
- Move into space expecting the ball to come back to you.

ONE-TOUCH WITH INSIDE OF FOOT_

If the ball to you has been hit slowly, using the outside of the foot is again a useful way of speeding up your team's play and can be done without having to check your running stride.

- Get your body into position by getting side-on to the ball.
- Keep your eye on the ball.
- Lock the ankle to ensure you generate suitable pace on your pass.
- Move into space expecting the ball to come back to you.

_ONE-TOUCH WITH OUTSIDE OF FOOT

I love a long pass, and practice makes perfect. Keep your eye firmly on the ball and make sure you get the right amount of height on your pass.

The long pass is not used nearly as often as the more common short pass with the inside or outside of the foot. But it is, nevertheless, a wonderful tool to have in your box. I recognize that it is harder for younger kids to come to grips with playing the longer pass, as they will struggle to get the ball into the air due to less strength in their legs than older kids, but that didn't stop me and I recommend that you start getting used to trying to play the ball through the air as accurately as possible from an early age.

It is important that you don't play the long pass for the sake of it. It's here that decision-making is vital. Take a second to look around you; would it be better for your team to play an easier, shorter pass and keep possession? If the answer to that is no, then great, play that long ball. It can be spectacular to watch and a nightmare for those defenders.

A good long pass will get defenders turning, will take the ball in behind them (they hate that), and will give an added dimension to a game that has become tight. Depending on how you hit the ball, you can make it travel 40 yards or so, and that alone is the most effective way of turning defense quickly into offense.

Before playing the pass, look up and assess whether a long ball is the correct option.

Remember, the target you are aiming for will be on the move and so aim for the space rather than the player.

The non-striking foot should be slightly to the side of the ball and behind it.

The striking foot should be locked at the ankle to ensure pace and the ball should be struck on its lower half to make sure you get it up in the air.

Keep your head still and your eyes on the ball and lean back slightly to get the ball up. It's vital to follow through and maintain that body position.

3

"IT IS IMPORTANT THAT YOU DON'T PLAY THE LONG PASS FOR THE SAKE OF IT."

2

_LONG PASS

A chipped pass is another smart option and can get you out of the tightest of situations. If there is an opponent in between you and the only teammate in space to receive the ball, the chipped pass will allow you to sail the ball over the defender's head. The backspin that you generate from this sort of pass means you don't need as much space as a long pass to make it work.

When chipping a pass, address the ball straight on (1).

The non-striking foot should be just to the side of the ball (2).

The striking foot should stab at the bottom of the ball (where it meets the ground), sending it into the air and over the nearby defender (3 and 4).

Keep your head still and your eyes on the ball.

CHIPPED PASS_

"LOOK FOR ACCURACY
RATHER THAN POWER."

Trying a back-heeled pass proves you are willing to improvise, and that is great. Don't, however, do it purely for show, as it is a pass you are making blind. Be aware of your teammate's position and if it is okay, go for it.

BACK-HEELED PASS_

Moving into space is vital when passing the ball, and if you collect a quick return ball from your teammate, defenses can be opened up quickly.

This is known as the one-two or the wall pass, when we play a ball to a teammate and immediately receive it back. This is a particularly clever way of getting behind rigid defenses and is at its most effective in the offensive third of the field.

The general concept is to play the ball to a teammate past a defender before moving forward and receiving the ball back.

It is crucial you play the ball at the right time. Ensure you are at a safe distance from the defender, not too close so your pass is blocked but not too far away, as the defender will be able to change his or her position.

Accuracy is vital.

Make sure the ball you play with the inside of the foot is perfectly weighted, as is the run you make to receive the return pass.

_ONE-TWO

This pass is useful as it won't always be possible to control a bouncing ball and therefore you need to be comfortable playing a pass in midair. You can volley this pass over the heads of nearby defenders as well as knocking it longer distances. As it is a pass that can be made early, defenders are immediately at a disadvantage.

When addressing the ball, make sure the body is relaxed.

Get the body positioned sideways to the line of the ball. Get the leading shoulder to relax and drop away to allow the striking leg a clean swing at the ball.

The non-striking foot should be well away from the ball to allow that clean swing to take place. This standing leg is vital here, as it must take the movement and rotation of the body.

The striking foot should face outward and the leg should swing forward and across the body.

Keep your head still and your eyes on the ball.

Remember to practice your passing with both feet. Look for accuracy rather than power and always listen to your teammates before passing the ball. You have more than one set of eyes on the field and they can tell you exactly what is okay and what isn't.

SIDE-VOLLEYED PASS_

After those bruising beginnings I was lucky enough to go on and achieve so much with United. To win so many trophies with the team I had idolized as a boy was so special and something I will always cherish. The first of those trophies came in 1996. United that season looked dead and buried as far as the Premiership was concerned, and at one point we were twelve points behind Newcastle at the top of the table.

The thing about United was that we didn't ever know we were beaten and would go and go until the bitter end. Gradually in 1996 we clawed ourselves back into the title race, beat Newcastle thanks to a goal by the inspirational Eric Cantona, and took the title, my first but United's third in four years. It was a wonderful feeling, but one that was about to increase with an FA Cup final against our archrivals, Liverpool.

The passion between both sets of fans is immense, and that day at Wembley, while far from being a classic soccer match, was my first real insight into the history between the two teams, and to win at the old ground (thanks to another Cantona goal) was unbelievable. My dad had taken me to countless FA Cup finals under the famous twin towers, and I would stroll up Wembley Way wondering what it would be like to be arriving there as a player. Now I was, and I was leaving with a winner's medal. Life was fantastic.

At the beginning of the following season, England's new manager, Glenn Hoddle, a player I had so admired as a boy for his fantastic range of passing, picked me for his first squad and for his first-ever team, in a World Cup qualifier in Moldova.

Pulling on that England jersey remains a huge

> "PEOPLE HAVE SAID TO ME THAT THEY NOTICED A CHANGE IN ME ONCE I BECAME CAPTAIN OF ENGLAND."

honor however many times you do it, but that first time is like a dream. You see those three lions and realize that all the hard work you have put in as a kid and a young pro have been more than worth it. My debut itself wouldn't have had too many fans jumping around their living rooms, but it wasn't that sort of game. We worked hard for a 3-0 win against a workmanlike Moldovan side. I had a hand in the opening goal, but that match wasn't about applause or praise. My England career had begun, and no one could take that cap away from me.

That cap, over the next eighteen months, was

SO MANY MEMORIES_

added to again and again. Glenn Hoddle liked what he saw in me and picked me for each game in the qualifying stages of the 1998 World Cup finals in France, but it would be across the Channel that I would have to deal with the first serious setback in my young career.

I have mentioned that as a pro, like anyone, you have to deal with the bad times. Maybe they are that much harder being splashed across the nation's newspapers, but when things went wrong in 1998 for me, I had people around me to help, people who cared, and that meant a lot.

Having been left out of the two opening games in the tournament, I had played my way back onto the team with a goal and a good performance against Colombia and was more than excited to face Argentina in what was billed the biggest of the second stage matches—and certainly the biggest so far of my young career.

It was a wonderful occasion. Our fans were in full voice and were being treated to a fantastic match that lived up to the hype that always occurs when these two sides meet. We recovered from going a goal down early on to actually taking the lead (thanks largely to a brilliant Michael Owen dribble and shot) before letting in an equalizer right at halftime.

The match was perfectly poised, but then, just minutes into the second half, came the infamous moment that would propel me to become the nation's public enemy number one. The Argentine midfielder Diego Simeone clattered into me from behind. As I lay on the floor, he pretended to ruffle my hair but instead pulled it and I lashed out, kicking him in the back of the leg. He of course dropped like a sack of potatoes and that was that: I was off. I had retaliated and had to learn the hard way that you simply cannot do that and hope to stay in the game.

"IT'S HOW YOU DEAL WITH
THE LOWS THAT CAN SHAPE
YOU AS A PLAYER AND AS
A MAN."

It was horrible. The sixty seconds from being shown the red card to walking off past my aggrieved-looking manager and down the tunnel will always remain with me. I can safely say that was the worst night of my life.

But it's how you deal with the lows that can shape you as a player and as a man. I had to get over that summer and quickly. I knew I would be in for some trouble when I got back to England but was advised by the likes of Tony Adams and Alex Ferguson that the best way to deal with those who set out to put me down was to work hard, play even better, and make them eat their words, and that's what I did.

The year 1999 will always be remembered at Manchester United as the most memorable of seasons. To come home from France like I did but to go on and win the Premiership, the FA Cup, and the Champions League just ten months later was an incredible turnaround in fortune for me and proves how important it is to shake off the lows and concentrate on what you do well, have faith in your

abilities, and remain focused on the job at hand.

With the Premiership won and the FA Cup taken once more, the team could concentrate on its biggest night in over thirty years. My dad had told me all about Matt Busby's great team that had been crowned European Champions in 1968 and now here I was, facing the mighty Bayern Munich of Germany for the honor of helping United back to the top of the European tree.

I was back in the Nou Camp, the field that I had visited as a pupil at Bobby Charlton's Soccer School, but this time I was a Manchester United player desperate to emulate the great man's achievements. What a night it turned out to be. We had a few injuries and suspensions and found ourselves a goal down for the majority of the game, but as I say, at United we really didn't know we were beaten and that attitude saw us claw back two goals in the last two minutes of the game. It was an incredible night full of drama, full of action, and ultimately full of glory. My first son, Brooklyn, had only just been born

those was being named captain of England. It was the year 2000. England had lost the last-ever game at the old Wembley, Kevin Keegan, had resigned and it was Peter Taylor who was given the role of caretaker-manager before Sven-Goran Eriksson's appointment.

I was woken one morning by my mobile phone and, not being the best morning person, answered the phone a little groggily until Peter Taylor greeted me and informed me that I would be captain of the team for the upcoming friendly against Italy. I thought I was still asleep. I'd always had ambitions of being named skipper of England, but ambitions don't always come true. This one had, and I was right on the phone again to Victoria, and my mum and dad, giving them the great news.

It may have only been a friendly, it may not have been the most prestigious or dramatic of occasions, but that night in Italy will always be with me. Leading your country out is something you can't describe. To put the armband on changes you. The chest swells with pride, and once more you are that boy in the park. It was something I wanted to do regularly, of course, and fortunately I have been able to do just that.

People have said to me that they noticed a change in me once I became captain of England, and I suppose when you are given such a huge responsibility, you do realize that it is time to live up to the task at hand. I suppose you could say it was time to really grow up.

I'd like to think that I proved over my first year as captain that I was up for it. Of course, there were those who thought it was not right that I had been given the job, and that is fine, it is a game of opinions. But as the team improved under Eriksson and we made strides to qualify for the 2002 World Cup, I felt I was growing into the role, and 2001 turned out to be one of the most memorable years for me in an England shirt.

My goal against Greece at Old Trafford remains such a special memory. It had been a topsy-turvy qualifying group, but we had turned it on its head

a couple of months earlier, but Victoria was there in the crowd to support me and that meant so much.

She had been there for me, along with my family, during the dark days the previous summer and now they were there in my finest hour. It had been the most draining of seasons, both physically and emotionally, but now it was over. We had swept the board and had won the biggest prize of all in the most dramatic circumstances of all. I think the club needed security to pry that famous trophy from my grasp that night. What a feeling.

Nights like that one in 1999 mean so much, and you can't beat the feeling of winning trophies. It's what we all play the game for and it's what excites all fans and players alike. You and your teammates work so hard to win things, and so when you do, the feeling of elation can't be matched. There have been, however, times when the highs in my career have been very personal: moments when all the dreams I had as a boy have reached fruition, moments that you only fantasize about as a hungry kid. One of

with that famous 5-1 win in Germany. It came down to the Greece game, a match that if we avoided defeat would see us traveling to Japan. Initially the occasion may have gotten to some of us as we found ourselves 2-1 down and needing a goal desperately.

In the last minute we won that free kick, and fortunately for me I managed to curl it in at the old Stretford End for what proved the most timely and crucial of goals. I could hardly talk after that match, such was the excitement within the camp and the adrenaline within me. That goal helped me win the BBC's Sports Personality of the Year award for 2001.

By the end of 2003, and having enjoyed so many of those highs in the red I had always cherished of Manchester United, it was time for a change. Barcelona had made it clear that they wanted me, which was a huge honor, but I hadn't discarded the idea of signing a new contract at United. Once, however, I heard that Real Madrid was also interested, there was only one thing to do—find the dotted line and sign my name.

Real Madrid is so massive, so prestigious, and so historical that I felt I had to join their team—and that's exactly what I did. What a club it is. Everything is on such a grand scale, and I remember the reception I got when I arrived in the Spanish capital was incredible.

My first game at the famous Bernabéu Stadium was like another dream. The fans, the noise, and the occasion were all so fantastic, as were the events on the field. It was a match against Mallorca and the Spanish equivalent to the Community Shield. We were brilliant. Raul and Ronaldo put us two up and then I got my head onto a cross and made it three. It was a magical moment, and one that immediately proved to me that I had come to the right place.

With so many wonderful memories (I have only mentioned a few), it is important that I don't forget the people, the games, and the goals that have shaped my career. I am ready for more, of course, but despite all the years in soccer, I make sure that today I have the same attitude in the job as I have always had.

I feel that I was brought up in the right way. From the age of three years old through to being a kid at

Manchester United, I was always taught to do things in a certain way and that is how I try to bring my own boys up. I was always told to treat adults with respect, to talk to them in the right way, and not to forget your "please" and your "thank yous."

Now that I am a little older I like to keep to those traits and remain very loyal to my family and also toward my job. Sometimes, I don't want to get out of my warm bed and go training when it's raining or snowing, but I do because I love the game so much and I am so motivated to go and learn and to further improve. I have been doing it now for twenty years and still love it. A lot of players don't enjoy the day-to-day ins and outs of training and would love nothing more than to just go and play the matches. One or two of us, however, like the daily grind of training, and fortunately I am one of them. It must stem from those days with my dad in the local park. Practice, practice, practice.

6

DRIBBLING_

Ask any of my teammates and they will tell you gladly that dribbling with the ball has never been my strong point. My method of making myself space hasn't been by beating my man. I have always preferred a good first touch, one that buys me the time I need before swinging in a shot or a cross.

No, dribbling at pace has never been a part of my game and at this point in my career I can safely say it never will be. You do, however, need to be able to make space for yourself and that means sometimes beating people with the ball. It can get you out of situations and open up defenses to take you in on goal.

You need to be comfortable on the ball, have a good change of speed, and if you can perfect the art of dribbling, you will become an automatic crowd favorite. Diego Maradona was the best dribbler I have ever seen, as he demonstrated against England

so famously during the 1986 World Cup. Today Ronaldinho has everyone on the edge of their seats, but at United I was lucky enough to play with Ryan Giggs, a player who used to get the ball and run at defenders knowing that they were scared of his skill and his pace. If you have that sort of player, a player who scares defenders, you will always create chances.

If you look at the greats, the players who would love to go at defenders and are forever running with the ball and improvising, they have a common factor: They aren't afraid of failure. If you look at creative people in general, they will happily fail at something

Make sure you become comfortable on the ball. Practice on your own—after all, when it comes to dribbling, who needs teammates?

if it means learning and improving for the next time.

By the way, before you all think I am completely useless at dribbling, I have had my moments. In 2003, Real Madrid came to Old Trafford for the second leg of a Champions League quarterfinal. Ronaldo had destroyed us with an incredible hat trick within an hour, but we never knew we were beaten at Old Trafford and we kept fighting to win the tie 4-3. Unfortunately it wasn't enough to take us through, but one of the two goals I got that night stands out.

I received the ball in a tight spot outside the area, and with quick feet I dribbled around Roberto Carlos and Guti before striking the ball cleanly into the top corner. It was a very un-Beckham-like goal, I suppose, but very satisfying. I was eating dinner with the Madrid team recently and that goal came on the television. I was quick to point my current teammates to the TV set. I hope I didn't put them off their food!

What will put a defender off their food is the idea of a forward running at them with the ability of beating them and putting them out of the game. While some teams can be successful by being organized, sticking to individual tasks, remaining rigid, and grinding down the opposition, most fans would love to see a team and a player who can improvise. This is where dribbling and an eye for the unexpected can be so important and entertaining.

To be able to penetrate in the final third is so important, and that is the same principle whether you are playing for Real Madrid or a local team in the park. Whatever level you are playing at, the team with players who are good dribblers and who are willing to beat players is the team that is going to enjoy success.

When attempting to dribble, how you approach the defender is vital. This will often be a slow run at the defender building into a medium pace, but you must be ready to explode past them. Keep the ball under control at all times, fake to make a defender go one way, quickly change direction, and you can

then throw in a trick or a turn before accelerating away. As you accelerate past the defender, try to cut across the defender's path. They will, especially in the final third of the field, be loath to make the challenge, as a free kick or even a penalty may well be awarded.

Managers and coaches won't mind at all if you try these moves in that last third. Here, the risk factor if you lose the ball is very low while the rewards if you succeed are extremely high. On the other hand, it is important to remember that the rewards for dribbling in your own defending third of the field are very minimal and the risk factor very high. Again, make the right decisions and your team will benefit.

Another important element to remember when thinking about dribbling is, it is not about "hogging" the ball. A good dribbler does it to aid their team's attacking options, not to make themselves look good. A good dribble allows a player to manipulate the ball, using different parts of their body, and enables the player to create openings where it seems there aren't any.

When dribbling, it is important to remember the following rules:

Always keep the head up. Running with your head down will only lead you into trouble. It is vital you can see oncoming defenders, your own teammates, and what possibilities you have. I have mentioned how important it is to make the right decisions when playing soccer, and running with your head up makes that possible.

Use different parts of the foot when dribbling. The inside of the foot, the outside, the heel, the toe, and the sole can all be used to manipulate the ball in a way that suits you and your team.

Use other parts of the body as well. The arms can be used for balance and also will keep the defender at bay. Dropping a shoulder or the head and faking to go one way before bursting the other will upset defenders, and that's what we are always striving to do, isn't it?

Keep the ball close to the body, but make sure it is out in front of the feet. If you are happy with the ball's location, you will be more comfortable making quick changes in direction and in speed.

Don't be afraid to have plenty of touches of the ball when dribbling. This keeps the ball firmly under control.

There are plenty of exercises that enable us to work on our dribbling.

Take four friends, each with a ball, and dribble within a small square marked out with cones. The trick is to avoid bumping into each other and each other's balls. Contrast the pace with which you move, make sure you are always turning, changing direction and using various parts of the foot. Spend time using only the inside, then the outside, of the foot, use the sole, and then dribble using only your weaker foot.

Always look up to avoid your friends. This will work on your close control and your ability to maneuver the ball and dribble out of tight situations.

Even when you're on your own, practice running with the ball at your feet and suddenly changing direction. Use the different parts of the foot to move the ball. Even with no one around, keep your head up so you get used to playing the game that way.

Generally get used to moving the ball around your feet. With your head up and facing outward, knock the ball with the inside of the right foot to the inside of the left and repeat between feet. As you progress, move around the field, changing the pace as you do so.

One of the best ways you can excel at dribbling is to watch your favorite players from the stands or on TV. When you play with your friends, try to copy a trick you've seen and don't be afraid if at first it doesn't come off. You can bet that the guy you saw dribbling so well with the ball is only so good at it because he has practiced for hours. Now it's your turn.

_DRIBBLING EXERCISES

At The Academy we offer kids from the ages of eight to fifteen the chance to visit, be it as part of the five-day soccer camps, the school day visits or the after-school clubs.

SCHOOL DAY VISITS

Here we want to give schools the opportunity to bring their pupils along for what we know will be an educational but thrilling day out of their classrooms. We want to inspire, educate, and entertain them.

A school day visit isn't just about soccer—it involves cross-curricular activities as well.

Of course, during the day, the visiting kids will enjoy the expertise of our world-class coaches and play plenty of soccer. They will learn about techniques and about tactics, they will play in a mini-tournament and leave—like my own boys when they came along—shattered but exhilarated. They will also have the chance—and this appeals to those kids who may not be as good at soccer as others—to participate in role challenges.

Soccer teams and the game itself are about far more than the guys like me who put on their cleats and get out there and play the game. A team or a club will have an army of people behind the scenes, helping the players and generally making things tick. Physical therapists, nutritionists, scouts, coaches,

THE ACADEMY: THE PROGRAMS_

fitness experts, equipment managers, and of course the managers themselves all have vital roles to play. While away from the team itself, the members of the press play a critical job in letting the public and the fans know about each team and each match. Each of these roles can be fulfilled by the kids at The Academy, but more of that later.

The day at The Academy is about encouraging a positive attitude toward sports and exercise in general. To do this we don't want to preach to the kids but let them take part, allowing them to see for themselves how fun soccer can be.

Currently we are adopting a World Cup theme to our school day at The Academy. The kids are split up into groups and are given different countries to represent. That team and its members can then go on and win bonus tokens, which convert into "goals," or points. The kids are encouraged to win these goals for their teams and can do so both on and off the soccer field. As well as being rewarded for good work with the ball at their feet, the kids can gain these bonuses for good sportsmanship, helping other students, showing good teamwork, and generally having a positive and helpful attitude.

"THE DAY AT THE ACADEMY IS ABOUT ENCOURAGING A POSITIVE ATTITUDE TOWARD SPORTS AND EXERCISE IN GENERAL."

Having been split up into different countries, they earn points and bonuses depending on how well they do. These are either gold, silver, bronze or, best of all, platinum tokens. They go into a warm-up before a team-building exercise. If you show good social skills, answer questions correctly, and generally help your team and its individuals, then you are constantly able to win more points. The idea is for kids to work as a team all the way through their day here.

They have coaching sessions and play games, all the while hopefully earning those bonuses for their team. The key to the whole day is the bonuses, because by trying to win those points they must show good team building and good spirit, offer good social skills, and help those who maybe aren't so good. We want the kids who come to The Academy to learn and to take from their visit good communication and leadership skills.

ONLINE SERVICES
WWW.THEDAVIDBECKHAMACADEMY.COM

We know that not all schools around the country can make it to The London Academy. Because of that we also offer teachers the chance to get onto our online service, an educational tool with customized content for teachers and students including lesson plans, educational games, and information centers with teaching units on soccer and health and fitness.

The idea is it becomes more than just a day trip for many who have been here, and for those who can't make it, their teachers can still give them a taste of what goes on at The Academy.

This helps teachers who, by their own admission, maybe aren't as qualified when it comes to soccer training. It assists those who need help coming up with some games, advice on how to troubleshoot a particular lesson, and how to identify talented kids.

SOCCER CAMPS

The soccer camps held over the various school holidays are based on the same principles as the school visits. Like the day visits, the camps are centered around the same World Cup theme and again the kids are split into different countries. We think that gives the trips an edge.

In the camps the cross-curricular stuff remains. They can do the classroom stuff and role-play at being the manager, the scout, press officers, coaches, fitness experts, nutritionists, and physical therapists. They can't play soccer all week long, so this offers an exciting and educational alternative.

On arrival each kid will receive their very own free Adidas kit before taking part in a schedule designed by some of the best coaches around. We hope that this is a once-in-a-lifetime experience for the kids who come here, and therefore we have tried to pull out all the stops.

As well as the role challenges, the best coaching, and a World Cup tournament, the kids will also take part in a skills circuit (more details of which can be found in the rest of this book). When I was at Bobby Charlton's school, we had a similar type of exercise, which I really enjoyed. I also won it and got to visit both Old Trafford and Barcelona's

Nou Camp, but it was great to test myself at all different aspects of the game such as short and long passing, dribbling, shooting, and heading.

AFTER-SCHOOL CLUB

This is all about soccer. Pure soccer. Kids can come by after school and get some great coaching. These sessions are all about playing the game. Again, these will be for players of all levels and are available for individuals or school or club teams and will focus once more on top-level coaching and allow for position-specific sessions (i.e., defending or goalkeeping).

THE
DAVID BECKHAM
ACADEMY™

THE
DAVID BECKHAM
ACADEMY™

TOURNAMENTS

In conjunction with Volkswagen, earlier this year we ran our first David Beckham Academy tournament in which clubs and schools from all over the country took part. The winners of each regional heat came down to The Academy to compete in the finals and the winner went on to compete in the Volkswagen Junior Masters Tournament in Germany, where they faced competition from teams from all over the world. We plan to build on this success and run more tournaments in the future.

As well as the competitive element this brings, kids, clubs, and coaches can enjoy interacting with others and can nurture links with other players and clubs from outside their usual environment. When I was a boy playing for the Ridgeway Rovers we used to travel abroad for various competitions and it makes you feel so special and gives you a real insight into what it is like to be a professional soccer player.

CORPORATE PROGRAMS

We want as many kids as possible to come and enjoy The Academy. To do that we are also offering corporate use to bigger kids who want to come along and use the facilities. We are of course situated on the edge of the world's largest financial district at Canary Wharf, so it makes sense that we make ourselves available to companies and institutions who can use what we have here for conferences, meetings, and client entertainment. We are also running coaching courses.

We can use the money that is made from big business and the coaching courses and pump it back into helping the kids. It is important to us all that the community gets as much as it can from what we do here. The Academy itself is investing in grassroots soccer—the sort of soccer that I myself grew up playing and learning so much from—as well as giving support to our partner charity, SHINE.

SHINE funds and develops educational initiatives that allow disadvantaged kids from London and Manchester extra attention and support to help them raise their achievement levels at school.

We are in a nice position where we can give something back. The kids that come here are really looked after. From the coaching they receive, to the facilities they find themselves in, to the food they are given to eat—it is all top notch and that means a lot, because that is our aim.

I guess what we want to do here, through these different courses, camps, and visits, is help kids to celebrate the game of soccer, the game I love. We want to promote an ethos that gives the kids the right attitude to losing and to each other. We want kids to identify with their teammates, learn about how to help each other as well as dribbling around a defender. We want to teach them about the right way of playing the game. How do you help someone on your team if they fail at something?

I remember in 2003 when I missed a penalty against Turkey, and while I was absolutely distraught I knew there was an important game to be played. I was captain of England, and I had to show that that miss hadn't got to me. As captain I have had to console guys who have felt they have let the team down, just as the likes of Tony Adams helped me in 1998 when I was sent off against Argentina. It's a team game, we are in it together, and we win and we lose together.

We have an obligation to those who come here to show them that sports and soccer can be great. Some kids will dread the idea of sticking on shorts and sneakers and taking part—they feel they don't fit in—but we can show them that they do, that they are wanted and can participate and contribute, and they seem to respond. Kids are very truthful. They'll let you know if things aren't good.

We want to make the day or the week unforgettable. They get certificates and medals to remind them of their visit. That's worked very well and we are proud that what they get from the activities is what stays with them, not the physical material things. Kids can gain from how they interact with each other and with what they learn. And you'll find there is very little disappointment from those who come.

We acknowledge and praise good play, but we want to make sure that all kids have targets, targets that they can reach and that leave them feeling great about their visit as well as themselves.

"KIDS CAN GAIN FROM HOW THEY INTERACT WITH EACH OTHER AND WITH WHAT THEY LEARN."

7

DEFENDING_

My old hero Mark Hughes used to say that when he, as an attacker, defended—and he was great at defending from the front—that the first thing he wanted to achieve when closing players down was to make that player drop his eyes and look down at the ball. When they are being forced to concentrate on the ball, they aren't looking up, can't pick out the right ball, and are aware that they may be tackled at any point. Today, Wayne Rooney is very good at that.

In Spain, the build-up is that much slower, so I have had to adapt and work on how I defend. In England the ball is often gone before you have a moment to position yourself. In England defending is that much more demanding, and I leave that to the experts like Gary Neville and John Terry.

I have never been the best at tackling, but I have tried to master the art of non-contact defending. By that I mean trying to manipulate where the opposing player with the ball can go, making his life awkward by positioning myself correctly and shepherding him into a space where he cannot cause me or my team damage.

If the fullback receives the ball from the keeper, I will go to that fullback and position myself in a way that forces the defender to play the ball in the middle of the field, rather than knocking a dangerous ball forward down the line. Once the ball is played inside, I will have support from the forwards, who can put pressure on the ball, maybe steal it away and go on to get a shot on goal.

You need to be able to read the game and your opponent and deny where you think they would like to go. As a team you can condense the play and keep your opponents under pressure.

What you are trying to do as a non-contact defender is often simply buy your team some time: Make the player with the ball slow his play down and allow your teammates to regroup and organize.

If I try to win the ball off a player ten times, I am

I have had to work hard on my defending. I remember in my early days at United—with me on the right and Ryan Giggs on the left—Alex Ferguson would say he had fourth division players on the team, in terms of work quality, with world-class talent. Defending is not something that comes naturally to me, but fortunately working at my game is, and so over the years I have knuckled down, put in the hard work, and made sure that the defensive part of my game is as good as it can be.

If you ask somebody to name the best defender in the world, invariably they will name a Paolo Maldini, a Rio Ferdinand, or a John Terry. Someone who plays across a back four. The thing is, some of the great defenders can be forwards who work hard to stop teams playing and, by closing down players from the front, are a very useful weapon for any team.

"SOME OF THE GREAT DEFENDERS CAN BE FORWARDS WHO WORK HARD TO STOP TEAMS PLAYING."

not going to win it ten times. What I might be able to do is make them do something that they really didn't want to do, such as go backward, sideways, put the ball out-of-bounds, or give up possession. These are degrees of success.

Midfielders and defenders, though, are a strange breed. The best ones love stopping goals. They will take as much pleasure from preventing goals as us attacking players do from scoring them. They need to be brave, they need to be fearless, but they also have to master the basics of defending. There will be times when a defender is in direct contact with play and will have opportunities to win the ball back for their team. To do this, they must be strong in the tackle and in the air, but that's not all.

Against the better players, they need to prevent a forward from turning, which means being close to that player all the time. It is imperative that they accept the fact that their opponent is going to get possession of the ball at times. When that does happen, they must prevent the player from turning. They can do that by being the right distance away so as not to invite being turned with a trick or a spin. A defender has done their job if the forward can only play the ball back from where it came. A defender can do their job, make the ball go back, and then rely on teammates to close down that secondary action.

A good defender will—and this can take time—be brilliant at making the right decision. They will read the game and know when to make a strong challenge and when to drop off, when to intercept and when to force the striker into a neutral position.

As I have said, for me defending is different. You aren't going to see me winning many headers against big center forwards, making last-ditch tackles, or throwing myself into challenges in the box. My game takes place on different parts of the field but that

Defending isn't only about tackling and heading. It's vital you know when to make your move. By holding your opponent up, your teammates will be able to regroup and any potential danger will be averted.

doesn't mean I don't need to do my part for the team.

For me personally, playing in midfield means I have a responsibility to stop the opposing team from building up their attacks from deep and I am fully aware that I can play a major role in stopping the ball from being played up to dangerous forwards. I can close down play, break up the rhythm of the opposition, and even win back possession for my team.

When the opposition has the ball, be that with their keeper or a defender, react quickly. Be on your toes and be ready to act.

When a fullback receives the ball, I will react quickly to that and sprint over to close him down. Ideally you should be on the move while the ball is in motion on its way to your opponent.

You should, however, slow your speed as you approach the ball. If you go sprinting into a tackle, your opponent will find it too easy to slip around using a fake or a sidestep. Keep control of your speed as you

"A GOOD DEFENDER WILL BE BRILLIANT AT MAKING THE RIGHT DECISION."

close them down and you will remain in control of the situation. Make sure you have good balance by staying low and in a slightly crouched position, keeping your head steady and edging in to close down the space.

Angle your position so that the player in possession can only go one way with their next pass.

You can gain the initiative. As they are trying to trick you, and therefore make space and time for themselves, you can do the same to them. Try your own fake, make like you are about to lunge in to a tackle, and make your opponent act. They may well look down at the ball—remember what Mark Hughes said about making the man on the ball look down—or even better, they may try to move the ball, giving you the chance to sneak in and take it from them.

> "BEING A GOOD DEFENDER MEANS BEING A CLEVER PLAYER."

It is vital that you don't dive in. The best defenders stay on their feet and will only get dirty and dive in as a last-ditch attempt to win the ball. Be patient and react only to the ball, not the player, as they will try to trick you with fakes and step-overs. Don't be fooled. When defending, it is important that you try to read what is going to happen next.

Patience is the key word. Time favors the player without the ball. The longer you stall your opponent, the fewer options they will have and the more time your team has to regroup.

I know that for a lot of young players, defending isn't at all glamorous. Many, me included, would rather be doing the so-called exciting parts of the game. They would rather be creating, dribbling, heading, and scoring, but those players must remember that the only way you can have the ball and do all those things is by winning it back from the opposition.

Don't wait or expect someone else to do that for you. By getting used to defending and enjoying defending, you will become a far better team player. Being a good defender means being a clever player, having good vision, good anticipation, and being very well organized. It isn't all about being a "stopper" or someone who just kicks the ball away from trouble. Defending is vital, can be creative, and is a skill we all must try to master wherever we play on the team.

_STAY ON YOUR FEET

When we were going through the design of The Academy, we immediately decided we needed two huge classrooms where kids can go, get on computers, watch different players, learn about the body, and learn about injuries and how to get over them. In the classrooms the kids enthusiastically play games, they work on tactics and technique, they can write press reports, and they learn about the human body, fitness, and nutrition. For me what happens in the classroom is just as important as what takes place out on the field.

Kids coming to The Academy with their schools are encouraged to answer mock advertisements for the different roles required. Of course, not every pupil will get their number one choice, but we do emphasize that each role is as important as the other and each individual is vital to their particular team.

TEAM MANAGER

Think you're the boss? Here we want someone who can make sure that their team has the best players money can buy. Each team's manager will be responsible for choosing who they think are the best players and that the squad is well balanced and a value for money.

The manager must understand the importance of different positions, different formations, and different skills as well as being able to make hard decisions, quickly.

The team manager should have a passion for soccer, be good at solving problems, and be good with money as well as numbers. It's all about managing a budget as well as a team. I've had a few great managers and I can tell you, the job doesn't look easy!

PHYSICAL THERAPISTS

There's more to it than just a magic sponge. You will be involved in the prevention and treatment of the many injuries that can occur on the soccer field. Having learned about the human body, you can advise players on how best to warm up and how they can take their heart rates, which change dramatically during a game.

The physical therapist will be interested in how the human body works, be eager to learn about our muscles and our bones, as well as be able to understand the link between heart rates and exercise. If you like helping your teammates, the medical side of the game, and solving practical problems, you might be the perfect physical therapist.

TEAM NUTRITIONIST

Grub's up! The team's nutritionist will be interested in what food and drink is best for players and athletes in general. You will be asked to sort foods out into groups and come up with menus that will make the players that much more energetic and better prepared for action.

The nutritionist should like good food, like to feel good, and be keen to learn how the two are linked. They should also be willing to share their findings enthusiastically with the team.

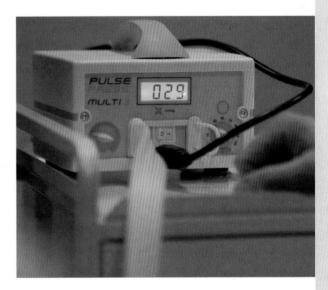

FITNESS COACH

Get those knees up! The team's fitness coach will learn all about different levels of fitness and what is the best advice and work for a player who wants to perform at the peak of their condition. Players aren't all that excited about being put through their paces, so you have to make sure you know what you are doing.

A good level of fitness is vital in soccer and the fitness coach must understand the importance of speed, strength, and flexibility. Do you like to be physically active, are you keen on learning more about health, fitness, and what makes a player like me tick? Then this job would be for you.

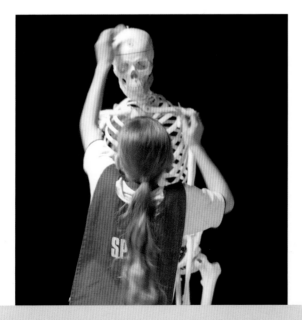

back on their various strengths and weaknesses.

You will learn about what makes a good soccer player, what to look for, and how to spot an emerging talent, however young they may be. I remember Malcolm Fidgeon, Manchester United's scout based in London.

"Lucky you had a good game," my mum said to me one day after a match for my district team.

"Why?" I asked.

"That man over there is a Manchester United scout. They want to have a look at you."

I guess you could say thanks to Malcolm, my story in soccer began.

TECHNICAL COACH

These are the guys who teach us all, however good we may think we are, to get better. Any player will always tell you that they are looking to improve, however well they're playing, and it is the coaches who help make that happen.

The coach will learn about tactics, different skills, and the best way to communicate what they have learned to the team members.

SCOUT

Can you spot a new talent among a crowd of other players? The team's scout is the unsung hero behind the scenes, taking in games all over the country, Europe, and the world to spot new talent. They also have to study teams that you may face and report

PRESS OFFICER

Stop the presses! The press officer has to be the mouthpiece between the team and the public. They must possess communication skills, be able to get down in words what they have seen on the field, have an eye for a catchy headline, and be happy in front of the camera. Over to you.

EQUIPMENT MANAGER

This is one for the younger kids who gets to design and look after the uniforms.

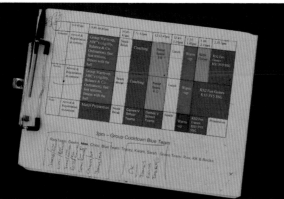

THE FUTURE

Ultimately we would like to be able to take The Academy out on the road. Yes, the facilities in South-East London are amazing, but what goes on inside The Academy is far more important than just how good it looks. We want to take what we do out to the kids, as we know not everyone can get here. We have a lot to offer and we want to be inclusive. We can't be that if we just lock ourselves away in a corner of Greenwich. We can take that wow factor with us as our coaches can offer kids, on their own doorsteps, a similar experience. It would mean we are getting to more and more kids, and that has to be a good thing. That's for the future.

We will also be running festivals of soccer alongside the tournaments. A festival is more about enjoying the game rather than winning, and both have their place.

The Academy's setting in South-East London is near enough to where it all began for me, and I guess you could say I've come home. This place is going to run for many, many years. I want my kids to come down here again and again, and I want to be coming here all the time after I've finished with the game. I just love seeing children enjoy The Academy, and it's something I look forward to doing for many years to come. Soccer, along with my family, has been my life. To me, The Academy is about giving kids a chance to share in that passion, a place for kids to learn, have fun, and take in the beautiful game.

Whatever you do in life, it is important to give yourself time off and to relax. That goes for us players too. For players there is plenty of time in the day when you are not training, and although I like to stay and practice alone after a session, I know how crucial some me-time can be.

I guess the stereotype of a soccer player winding down from his work is on the golf course. I've never really been into golf, but I wish I had the time to get out and play a round of eighteen holes. When you have three very energetic young boys to look after, there is little else you can do with your free time.

Having said that, being with my family is far from a grueling chore. I love spending time with my wife and kids. After a hard day's training or after being away with the team, I long to come back to the house, see Victoria, and play with the boys. To me that is relaxation time, and I would have thought far less infuriating than trying to master the game of golf!

When you are a soccer player, people often don't realize that you are away from home and from your family a lot. For the season, you are at work far more than you are not and that means I don't get to see Victoria and my boys half as much as I would like. Because of that, the time I do have with them is wonderful and I cherish every moment.

The boys love The Academy. They've been a few times and think Daddy's new soccer school is way cool. Every time we come back to London, they ask, "Can we go to The Academy, can we play soccer at The Academy?" I remember the first time they came and were running around for hours on end. They were dripping in sweat, and that night I don't think they have ever slept so well. Now they know how Daddy feels every day!

As well as my family, I enjoy other passions away from soccer. I have always enjoyed clothes, fashion, and style. I'm not saying I have always had good style, but from an early age I was keen on dressing up in a way that didn't necessarily fit with the norm. Maybe it came from my mum being a hairdresser.

I like to feel comfortable and throw on a pair of jeans, a T-shirt, and some sneakers, but I do love to dress up and try to look my best. Funnily enough, my son Romeo is exactly the same; even at such a young age he loves to make an impression.

MORE THAN A SOCCER PLAYER_

Whenever we go out for dinner, he's pestering us to let him wear a suit. I think it's great. He must get that from his dad.

As well as fashion, I also love music. People keep saying that with the England squad I am the resident DJ, but that's just not true. I don't know where that one came from. We have a stereo when we travel together and yes, I do have loads of music to take away with me and to play in the locker room and on the bus, but no way am I the sole DJ. I wish!

With players like Jermain Defoe and Rio Ferdinand around, there is no chance of only one DJ. With those guys and me there is a lot of R&B and hip-hop, as you can imagine, but Gary Neville sometimes takes over and plays his indie stuff. Gary is a good Manchester boy and loves Oasis, which is cool, but usually he has to bow down to the majority and that means listening to our stuff.

When I finish with England duty, and with all that music ringing in my ears, it is lovely to come home. For the last three years, home has been Spain's capital, Madrid. What an adventure it has been and despite the upheaval we have loved it.

It wasn't an easy decision. On the soccer side of things, obviously Real Madrid was as big as you get, but I also had to think of my family. It's a great upheaval leaving your home country, and it was something we weren't going to do lightly. Fortunately my wife was very supportive; she knew how much a move to a club like Madrid would mean to me, and so we went for it.

I have experienced a different way of playing soccer and played for a huge team in a soccer-mad country like Spain. I have had to adapt, and it hasn't been easy to come to terms with the climate or the language. My children, however, have grown up in another country, gone to very different schools, met different kids, and learned a different language. My boys now speak and understand Spanish, and I would have loved to have had that as a child. I won't lie, I have found the language hard, but I do get by. I understand what is being said, I can read the newspapers, but I am far from fluent. As a family we love it, though.

As for the training in Spain, it has been in stark contrast to what I was used to and brought up on in England with United. It took a lot of getting used to, but what I have been able to take from my time overseas is the wonderful players I have worked alongside. The different techniques I've encountered have taught me a lot. I have worked with players such as Raul, Roberto Carlos, Ronaldo, and Zinedine Zidane, so you can only learn from these guys and take positives from their wonderful talents. All of these players have shown an interest in my Academy, and I hope to have some of them over as guests one day.

It's not only great soccer players I have been lucky enough to mingle with. Through my time in soccer I have met some other sporting greats and heroes, such as the wonderfully inspirational Muhammad Ali, and Michael Jordan, whom I have always admired. Away from sports I have met Madonna, who surprised me when she seemed to know who I was—well, that I was a soccer player, anyway. Perhaps the biggest thrill was meeting Nelson Mandela when England traveled to South Africa in 2003. It was a very humbling experience. What an incredible man—the father to a nation, and amazingly cool with it.

So, now I am back in London with The Academy. You could say I've come full circle. London's where I'm from, it's my manor and where I was brought up. I left home when I was sixteen to join Manchester United and have lived away for fifteen years now, but it will always be home. People are always surprised when I tell them I am from London, "You must be from Manchester," they say, but they are wrong and the capital is a massive part of my life.

I spent those first sixteen years of my life there, part of me will always be there, and I am always going to live there when my playing days are over. There are other places that I'd like to see and even live, but the one place I will always go back to is London. Because of that, London is the right place to have the flagship Academy. Definitely.

I wish to continue to play at the top level for as long as possible, but the reality of life, however, is that there will come a day when I am no longer playing the game I have always cherished. Not professionally anyway. So what then? Well, the academies and my family will take up a lot of my time, of course, but I will also be involving myself far more in a cause that I treat incredibly seriously, and have done so for a number of years.

When I was at Manchester United, I was asked to work with UNICEF. The club had close ties with the children's organization and it was my pleasure to lend a hand. A few of the players, including Ryan Giggs, and I went to a Thai orphanage during a club tour to the Far East, and it had a tremendous effect on me.

In 2004 I received a personal letter from the United Nations General Secretary Kofi Annan, asking me to become a goodwill ambassador. I was so honored, and of course I said yes. I jumped at the chance and have done my best to help out with the Asian tsunami relief and recently did some work with Robbie Williams for AIDS awareness.

As a soccer player, it is hard to get a good stretch of days off, but when I retire I plan to have a much more hands-on role as ambassador and can't wait to get out in the field, helping in whatever way I can. It's an incredible charity and one that makes me very proud to be associated with.

8
CROSSING_

It was Pele who said soccer was nothing without goals, and I'm not going to argue with the great man. I love the feeling of scoring goals. The adulation from the crowd and your teammates is amazing, but—and I've had this from a very young age—I get as much satisfaction from helping create a goal, and since those early days playing in the park, I have always enjoyed getting the ball into the box and setting up strikers.

Crossing the ball into the danger area has been a massive part of my game; it's probably what most people associate me with, a trademark, if you like. When I was a kid, I loved to watch Gordon Strachan at Manchester United. He was a clever player who would, through his ability to cross the ball, create so many chances, and to me that seemed as exciting as actually scoring the goal itself.

Once I had followed in Gordon's footsteps and was lucky enough to play for United, I would run that same right wing and look to get the ball into the box as quickly and as effectively as possible. Getting the ball into the penalty area can cause havoc in even the most organized of defenses, and since those early days I have taken great pleasure in my time with Manchester United, Real Madrid, and England in setting up goals from wide areas for my teammates.

At United, when we scored from one of my crosses, the fans would immediately chant the name of the scorer, but then right away it would be my name they were singing, "There's only one David Beckham!" and that felt great.

In 1999, one of my most unforgettable years in soccer, United faced the mighty Inter Milan in the quarterfinal of the Champions League. When two clubs like United and Inter Milan clash in a tournament like that, there is always going to be massive hype. A lot of that that year centered on me and Inter's Argentinean international Diego Simeone. It was the first time that the two of us had clashed since the fateful World Cup match the previous summer, in which I had been sent off.

It was a classic Old Trafford night. There's something about European nights at the old place that would send shivers down your spine, and with the crowd right behind us we ran out 2-0 winners, thanks to two fine headers from Dwight Yorke. He was in great form that year, but that night was especially memorable for me as I set both of Yorkie's goals up with what turned out to be pinpoint crosses. It was an occasion that will always stay with me, not only because of my crosses and the result, but my oldest son, Brooklyn, was born the next day.

Playing wide on the right means I have always got into positions where my best option was crossing the ball into the box, so it was very important that from a young age I was comfortable in doing so. The key for me, though, is making sure I vary the sort of cross I put in. The defenders know I am going to cross the ball; it's what I do best, so it is up to me to leave them guessing and wondering about exactly what sort of cross I am going to put in. I can vary the pace of the cross, the position of the cross, and its height.

Sometimes it can be interesting to think about the cross you are going to send in from the other side of the fence. What sort of cross is going to upset and worry the defenders? Make life difficult for the defender by making sure they have to think and work if they are to have any chance of clearing it.

When thinking about your crossing, try to get to know the penalty area and the best places to put the ball. There are different "zones" in the box, each of them as dangerous as the other. If you can find these zones consistently, you will cause trouble, and it is then up to your attackers to make themselves available to score.

One zone is at the near post, one is central, one is the deep area at the back post, and one is slightly farther out but again toward the back post.

As a youngster, begin with concentrating on your accuracy. As you get older and used to crossing, you will find that the power and the height required will come, but start with getting the ball to go exactly where you want it.

Line up cones just outside the 18-yard box, running toward the bye line. Start by dropping a shoulder; touch it past one cone. Make sure the first touch takes the ball out from under your feet, take a look up into the box, and then concentrate on the delivery.

In time, make sure you go for pace as well as accuracy so that you reach your intended target. In tennis and golf, they say that the good players know when they have hit a good shot just by instinct. In soccer, the more you practice, the more

you instinctively know, just by the way the ball leaves your foot, that it's a good ball in. Once you master that and send in good delivery after good delivery, it's up to your forwards to get on the end of your cross.

I have never worried about crossing the ball as early as possible. I like to generate enough bend on the ball to send it in from any angle, but you will often find yourself at the bye line, a position where many crosses are sent in from.

In England, ask any grandparents and they will tell you about the good old days when the likes of Stanley Matthews and Tom Finney would race down the wings, leaving defenders in their wake before sending in a cross for their giant center-forwards to nod home. Today in the Premiership, players such as Damien Duff, Matthew Etherington, and my old pal Ryan Giggs are experts at getting fast to the bye line before getting a dangerous ball into the box. Defenders hate having to deal with a ball that comes flying across their area. Here are some methods of causing the maximum damage.

"GETTING THE BALL INTO THE PENALTY AREA CAN CAUSE HAVOC IN EVEN THE MOST ORGANIZED OF DEFENSES."

This is my favorite type of cross. You can send this cross in early and, when done well, it can cause havoc in the penalty area.

A whipped cross, sent in at full speed, that isn't in the air for long and doesn't give the defender time to make decisions, is often the most deadly and effective.

Make sure when you receive the ball that your first touch is a confident one and that you take the ball out of your feet so you can run onto the cross (1).

You want to get swerve on the ball, as you want that cross to whip in (2). To achieve this, wrap your foot around the ball on contact, striking the bottom half of the ball to get it off the ground as swiftly as possible (3).

A good defense, as soon as you receive the ball and are readying yourself to send in the cross, will send a defender to the near post to deal with the ball. Make sure you clear that first defender. Whatever cross you put in, this is the most important rule. Clear that first defender.

Send the ball in fast between the keeper and the defender, leaving one of them having to make a decision about how to defend it. This can cause mass confusion and give your striker the opportunity to get in and score.

_WHIPPED CROSS

1

CHIPPED CROSS_

This can be a risky cross. Not only do you have to clear that first defender, you also need to make sure you completely bypass the other defenders in the box, and (this is the hard part) the keeper too.

Get onto the ball quickly, making sure again that your first touch is a good one.

The ball needs to get into the air quickly in order to miss all of those obstacles, so you must make sure you chip the ball with enough power to generate the height required (1). Like when you chip a pass, strike the ball with a stabbing movement, hitting the ball at its base where it touches the ground (2 and 3). Because you have to send that pass quite a distance, do this with an adequate amount of force (4).

"AS A YOUNGSTER, BEGIN
WITH CONCENTRATING ON
YOUR ACCURACY."

This is a very exciting cross. When done at pace this is a cross that will have fans off of their seats and defenders pulling out their hair. If you have beaten a couple of defenders and find yourself at the bye line, this is often the best option.

If you send a deep ball to the back post, you will have to bypass a number of obstacles to get there. Defenders and the goalkeeper will have to be beaten by your cross, and that, as I have mentioned, is going to be tough. The better ball from the bye line can be the cutback, for an intelligent oncoming attacker to meet and get their shot away.

Paul Scholes was superb at these, and I would on countless occasions look up to see Scholesy hanging back while defenders and strikers were rushing into the box. He would then come late into the box and I could cut the ball back toward the penalty spot and lay on the ball for him to score.

For this cross to work, it is vital that you look up before playing it. There is no point pulling the ball back if no one is there.

Having seen your target, cross the ball using the inside of the foot. This cross doesn't depend on major power; in fact it is more important that you are accurate, and you don't want to overhit it.

Aim for the penalty spot, ensuring you have the right pace on the ball.

THE CUTBACK_

I have always enjoyed taking corners and have done so for all my clubs and my country. Corners are a major source of goals and, when executed properly, are vital to a team's hopes.

The in-swinging corner is the most effective type of corner. Here, you can send the ball in at extreme speed and with the amount of bodies in the box, anything can happen.

Strike the ball on its bottom half, wrapping your foot around it to achieve that swerve and pace.

As ever, make sure you clear the first defender.

Ideally you want to send the ball into the six-yard box between head height and the crossbar.

When out-swinging the corner, you can go for accuracy rather than pace, and this gives you a chance to vary your delivery. One I particularly like sending in is aimed for the edge of the 18-yard box for a player to meet and volley at the goal. If it comes off, it is really spectacular.

_CORNERS

Soccer players like to think of themselves as master craftsmen, and therefore are obviously going to take pride in their tools. That's why I, for one, have always taken a keen interest in the cleats I wear and to this day have a great relationship with the guys at adidas, who make my footwear. I remember, when I was a kid, just how great it felt to get a new pair of cleats. I'd spend hours cleaning and polishing them in order to get them just right for a match. I guess nothing has changed there. Simon Wright works for adidas, and he'll tell you about how together we come up with the cleats you see me wearing for both Real Madrid and England:

"David is very hands-on when it comes to his soccer cleats," says Simon, "and we at adidas like to encourage that input. David's cleats always reflect his unique sense of style and, in order to achieve that, we always listen to his ideas.

"We obviously need to ensure that the fit of the cleats is perfect for David. This we achieve by

working with the molds we have of David's feet. We have plenty of those, of course, but we do like to remold the feet every now and then to check for the smallest changes. David has had knocks and injuries to his feet, and these can reshape the foot. Those changes can affect the fit of the shoe, so we like to keep a regular check on that.

"Aside from the fit, the design of the cleats is obviously a key priority. At the start of the process, we come to David with a number of conceptual ideas and sketches of how we envisage his next cleat to look. We like to bounce those ideas off David and give him the rationale behind our thinking. Because of that constant dialogue with David, we can get an idea of where he is coming from and what the cleat should represent.

"The adidas Predator cleat and technology suits David's game and aids that vicious swerve he likes to get through the ball. He is our key player when it comes to Predator, and because of that we like to keep his cleats unique.

"With that in mind, the first thing we will look at is the color, something that is very personal to David.

"David's cleats have definitely become famous for how personal they are to him, and he has always asked to have his boys' names on the cleats.

"Upon agreement of the design, color, and detailing, the cleats are then put into the sampling process. We then review the first samples with David, agree upon any necessary amendments, and create a finalization sample. This is then approved and we put all the necessary measures in place to be able to commence production.

"In essence, from presenting first ideas to delivering the final cleat to both David and consumers, we are looking at a time scale of about sixteen months."

IT'S ALL IN THE CLEATS_

9
FINISHING_

I don't care what level you're playing soccer; you could be in front of 80,000 fans in the world's top stadiums, watched only by a man and his dog on your local field, or just with your friends using jackets for goalposts. Wherever you are, you just can't beat scoring a goal. For me, seeing the net bulge and hearing the roar of the crowd has always given me such a huge buzz. I have always loved working on my shooting, and while I am far from a natural finisher, I am confident in having a go at keepers from all sorts of angles and from all sorts of ranges.

There's nothing the fans love more than seeing a player shape to shoot, head, or volley the ball toward the goal. The biggest and loudest of crowds can be silenced by that split second before a strike on goal. That raw excitement cannot be matched within the game of soccer; it literally takes your breath away.

The act of finishing and scoring goals is far from easy, but some players make it look all so easy. I have been lucky to play with some of the best in the business—players who take it all in stride, confidently taking chance after chance.

"SEEING THE NET BULGE AND HEARING THE ROAR OF THE CROWD HAS ALWAYS GIVEN ME SUCH A HUGE BUZZ."

Ruud van Nistelrooy at United was one such player, as is Ronaldo at Real Madrid, while Thierry Henry at Arsenal is another who makes the art of goal scoring look merely effortless.

To these players, finishing is all about instinct. Sure, they have to practice at it, but they seem to have the knack of simply finding the one part of the goal that the keeper cannot cover.

Finishing, though, isn't only for forwards. Players in all positions should feel confident about getting a strike in at goal. It's about technique and, once again, all about practice. Even defenders, while they are not going to always be near enough to go for a goal, should be competent at both shooting and especially headers, as they will have the chance to attack set plays and corners.

This is a very hard discipline. You've beaten the last defender, you're through with only the keeper to beat, but now it gets tough. The crowd hushes as you approach and you must keep your nerve, outwit the goalie, and score that goal.

Some players show supreme confidence and make this look so easy. English dads will tell you about Jimmy Greaves who would make a one-on-one look like a stroll in the park. Today, those players I have already mentioned thrive on the pressure. It's all about remaining calm, making up your mind early, and somehow managing to almost pass, or even caress, the ball into the net. That's what guys from Greaves to Henry are able to do. These quality strikers will appear to have loads of time. It can appear to us fans that these players have slowed down, taken the heat out the situation, but in

actual fact they are still moving at pace but have the ability to carry out the movement comfortably and without fuss. That's when a goal is scored.

One-on-one finishing is not my strength. I don't like running at the goal with only the keeper to beat. Give me a long-range strike any day. Personally I am not that comfortable going past goalkeepers; you will usually find me trying to chip the keeper or lob him before he can steal the ball off me.

For attacking players, however, it is a very important skill to master. Feeling comfortable while running at goalkeepers is a must for all forwards and is something they actually relish. With practice you can eventually feel so confident that you just won't believe you are going to miss. If you have faith in your ability, the keeper's actions should never hinder that belief.

When you receive the ball, run at pace so as to get away from the last defenders.

Take the ball at an angle toward the goalkeeper. The keeper will try to stay up on his or her feet for as long as possible. They won't want to commit themselves, so keep a clear head. They want you to panic, so don't!

Disguise your actions by turning your body to the side. You can also use your eyes to sell the keeper and kid them to exactly which way you plan to go.

Having committed the keeper to one side of the goal, slip the ball into the opposite corner.

With more practice and confidence, you can attempt other options, such as dribbling the ball around the keeper or delicately chipping it over a diving goalie.

 _ONE-ON-ONE

There are those, however—like me, for instance—who prefer to scream the ball into the net. As I say, I'm far more comfortable in striking the ball from a distance. I love it and always have.

My advice to young players is, when it comes to shooting, concentrate on accuracy before power. The power will come in time, but if you can master aiming for the corners of the net (the places that keepers find it hardest to stop your shots), you will have gone a long way to becoming a thorn in a goalkeeper's side.

I know I go on about practice and how vital it is, but that's simply because it *is*. We all love to shoot, though, and practicing your shooting should be really fun. When practicing, make sure you are striking the ball in the right way. Use the instep of the foot to generate power and accuracy.

The instep is basically the laces of the cleat. This ensures most of the foot is behind the ball, and it is here that most goals originate from.

Approach the ball at a slight angle.

If striking the ball with your right foot, point the left shoulder toward the target.

The non-striking foot should be planted next to the ball, pointing toward the goal. It should not be too far away from the ball, but not too close so as to hinder the striking foot.

Get the body over the ball.

Strike the ball with the instep.

If you want to keep the ball along the ground, strike the ball through the center or top half of the ball. If you want to get the ball up (if you are aiming for the top corner, for instance), then strike the ball through the ball's bottom half.

Keep the head steady and looking down at the ball.

To generate more power, both feet should leave the ground on the moment of impact (Bobby Charlton was especially good at this technique).

Follow through with both the striking foot and the body.

POWER SHOOTING_

Once you feel more confident with your shooting you can begin putting it into practice within game situations, and that means shooting from a distance. There may be times when you would be better off passing to a teammate in a stronger position, but often your best option will be to shoot. Don't be afraid to miss, because sometimes you will. But an ability to strike from a distance can be a fantastic weapon for both you and your team.

This is a part of the game that has always come naturally to me. I love shooting, I love scoring goals, and the vast majority of my goals have come from outside of the box. My style of shooting means I am able to fake the keeper into going one way and hopefully bend it the other. I am comfortable going for both corners and like to think I can test a keeper from most angles.

That's not me being big-headed. The reason I feel so confident about that aspect of my game is because, from a young age, I have practiced so much on that particular skill. It was actually a goal from a distance that convinced me that I had finally arrived as a professional player. With one memorable goal, I was suddenly being talked about on television and in the stands. It was a fantastic moment and one I will never forget.

I shot from within my own half. I'm not saying you should always try to shoot from so far out, but on this occasion, I looked up, saw the keeper off his line, felt confident, and had a go. Sometimes it pays to try the unexpected.

It was the first game of the 1996/97 season and United was playing Wimbledon in South London on a sunny August afternoon. I had only just become a regular, and we were in fine form and comfortably two goals up as the game entered injury time. Brian

"TIME YO
AND WORK
SPRING Y

I'm usually putting the ball onto heads
heading it, but that's not to say I don't
my forehead dirty. Having said that, a l
young and old, don't like to head the ba

Younger kids should be encouraged
ball using a softer ball. Get used to how
you get the technique right, you shouldn
about the ball hurting you, and instead i
another way for you to hurt a defense.

You can practice that technique by sir
in pairs with a friend and heading the ba
each other as if playing tennis. See how i
and for how long you can keep the ball u
trying to beat your record and, in time, yo
that you are far more comfortable using y

When heading the ball:

• Be brave. This is an important part of the
not something to be afraid of.

• Make sure you meet the ball with your fo
ensure maximum control.

• Time your jump and work on the spring y

Try to head the ball down and aim it the
way that the ball has come to you. This will
the keeper is off-balance.

_HEADIN

McClair rolled the ball into my stride and, as I
approached the halfway line, I had a look up and saw
the keeper way off his line. Would I have shot if it
had been 0-0? Who knows? I would like to think that
I would have. As I say, those who are willing to
improvise in soccer can often cause the most damage.

I struck the ball—I later heard that my manager
Alex Ferguson groaned as I hit it—and it sailed
through the air for what seemed an age before
evading the keeper's desperate attempts and
dropping into the net. It was a wonderful moment.
Not a game-winning moment, but one that filled me
with confidence.

Most of our shots, though, are not from our own
half, but there will be plenty of moments when a
strike from a distance is a very strong option.

First of all, take the ball early. It may be coming to
you at an awkward angle or on your unfavored foot,
but if you let it run onto your stronger foot, the
chance may have gone, so you have to be prepared
to take the moment early.

Check where the goal is and then concentrate on
your contact. If you get that right, nine times out of
ten you will have success. By success I mean you will
make the keeper work. When striking at the goal,
make the keeper work. You may not score, but if the
keeper is forced to make a save, who knows what
can happen.

If you know you have the ability to make the ball
move and to make the keeper work, you won't think
twice about shooting, and that can buy you the split
second to get a better shot away.

These are the main principles to follow when
practicing your shooting:

At first, concentrate on your accuracy. Use the
inside of the foot and pass the ball into the net. In time

you can start looking for power, using the instep. Aim
for the corners of the goal, keeping the ball low.

• Don't be afraid to miss. When practicing your
shooting, place cones outside of the posts as "near
miss targets." Give yourself three points for a goal,
and one point for striking the post. This will
encourage you to aim for the corners.

• Just before striking the ball, look up to see where
the keeper has moved to. This may have a bearing
on where you want to place the ball.

• Keep your body over the ball and don't lean back.

• Place the non-striking foot firmly next to the ball,
pointing toward the target.

• Use your arms for balance.

Try experimenting with different parts of the foot.
The outside of the foot, for example, gives added
swerve and is an alternative to the instep.

Stay calm, keep the head steady, and get ready to
celebrate!

_SHOOTING FROM
A DISTANCE

As I mentioned earlier, there will b[...]
simply won't have time to assess [...]
the ball on your favored foot, and [...]
Soccer is a fast game, and the bett[...]
quickly to stay one step ahead of t[...]
Being able to volley the ball is a pe[...]
this. If you have the confidence to [...]
means you won't have to wait to co[...]
giving the defenders time to close y[...]
the ball is played through the air tov[...]
simply strike it before it drops, and t[...]
the best of keepers. If you make the [...]
connection, the power generated wil[...]
shot is an incredibly hard one to sav[...]

A good volley is all about good tec[...]

• Ensure a solid connection by keepir[...]
  the flight of the ball all the way to y[...]
• Keep the non-striking foot firmly on[...]
• Use your arms for balance.
• Keep your knee over the ball.
• Rotate your hips.
• Follow through with the kicking leg t[...]
  power.

For even more spectacular results, c[...]
to try the overhead kick (or bicycle kick[...]
most spectacular of attacking volleys a[...]
will, even if unsuccessful, get fans out o[...]

• As the ball arrives through the air with[...]
  to the goal, lean back, putting your we[...]
  non-striking foot.
• The striking foot should be at full stret[...]
• Bend the non-striking foot and launch [...]
  the air.
• You should connect with the ball using t[...]
  the cleat.

Keep the arms outstretched and ready to [...]
fall. If done incorrectly, this can be painful[...]

Moving to Spain has helped me so much both on and off the field. In moving my family away from comfortable England, Victoria, the boys, and I have all had to adapt to a different culture, a different lifestyle, and that has enhanced me as a person. As for me the soccer player, I have had to improve and learn, and now feel I am a far better player technically.

I have yet to win anything in Spain, and last season was another frustrating time. When you're not picking up trophies, it can be a tough place to be –the mentality here is that Real Madrid must win things; that is their ethos, that's what they have always done.

As a team we more than accept that and each season we feel we are going to achieve our goals. You have to keep that belief. It has been hard, especially with our fierce rivals Barcelona running away with everything, including the European Cup. We have to get on with it and knuckle down and, as I say, believe that this coming season will belong to us.

That will to achieve can mean pressure, but a big plus for me has been just how welcome the Madrid locals and the fans have made me and my family feel. They are renowned for being a hard set of fans to please, but if you perform, play well, show them that you are as hungry for success as they are, and that you are willing to do your best in every game, then they will take to you. The Bernabeu is an incredible place to play soccer when you have the support of the fans.

In Spain, my life outside of the game is pretty normal, boring even. I get up in the morning and drive to training. En route I pick up my coffee, the usual every morning, and then it's down to work.

Away from the game I will spend time with the boys, pick them up from school, play with them like any dad would, and spend time with Victoria. The two of us have fallen in love with Spain. We like the food and we love to go out to small but very Spanish restaurants. Madrid is a very romantic city, and we like to take advantage of that fact as much as possible by going for dinner and enjoying where we live.

The key for us is how friendly the people of Madrid have been. They immediately made us welcome, they immediately helped us feel at home, and we couldn't begin to thank everyone for that.

The thing is, I'm not the sort of person who has to be busy. I put a lot into my soccer, so away from the field I am more than happy taking it easy. I like to put my feet up, relax, and rest. Having said that, with three boys to contend with, that's not always the easiest thing in the world to do!

The year 2006 saw me take part in what was my third World Cup. Where does the time go? We qualified without too much fuss, although there was the usual criticism after a defeat in Northern Ireland, a game that saw me play a more central role. To be honest, I wasn't bothered about all the talk regarding where I should play. I know I can do a job either in the middle of the field or out on the right, so I just get on with things. People will always say I am better on the right because I put crosses in, and maybe that is true, but I still enjoy fulfilling both roles and feel I can do a job wherever I am asked to play.

The best thing about going into the World Cup in Germany was how fit and strong I felt. In 2002 I had so many concerns about my foot—would I make the games, how fit was I going to be?—and that tarnished what should be the most exciting time for any soccer player. This year I was able to forget about peripheral worries and concentrate on the

soccer and captaining my country. I was fresh and ready to play, and that just added to my enjoyment. I can tell you that it doesn't matter if it is your third World Cup or your first, whether you are young or old, the thrill you get from being there never subsides. It's the pinnacle, and to be involved is such a buzz.

We had huge arcades set up in the hotel to help pass the time, but I'm not a huge computer game man, to be honest. You'd always find the youngsters in there, and while I would pop in from time to time, I was more than happy watching DVDs and getting as much rest as possible. As captain there is always something to do, something that needs to be done, like press conferences. It can be tough at times, but that is the captain's role.

Soccer has been my passion. Throughout my life, soccer has meant so much to me and I have been fortunate enough to realize so many of my boyhood dreams. Playing for the greatest clubs in the world and representing my country in three World Cups has been incredible.

The 2006 World Cup didn't finish as we would have liked. We were all devastated not to go further in Germany, but for me it was a privilege to captain what I maintain is a truly great set of players.

After the Portugal defeat in the quarterfinals, I stepped down as England captain, something I found very hard to do. Let me tell you, you don't give up that armband without very serious consideration. I had spoken to my family and those closest to me, and we agreed that the time was right. It has been the greatest honor of my life to captain my country, and leading the team out on those 58 occasions was something I will never forget.

Although it was a disappointment to hear that I am not part of Steve McClaren's squad at present, I am determined to show that I can still perform at the highest level for my country. I'm looking forward to an exciting season ahead with Real Madrid under the new coach, Fabio Capello.

"I WAS FRESH AND READY TO PLAY, AND THAT JUST ADDED TO MY ENJOYMENT."

10
FREE KICKS AND PENALTIES_

Free kicks have been good to me. Over the years I have loved practicing, trying to perfect, and scoring free kicks for my clubs and my country. I guess my most famous free kick was in 2001 against Greece at Old Trafford, when my last-minute strike secured the country's place in the 2002 World Cup Finals in Japan.

There was only a minute or so left and we were rewarded a free kick about thirty yards out. I remember placing the ball down, with 60,000 fans willing me to score. All I could think about was that I had had seven or eight free kicks beforehand and not got close with one. It was a huge occasion and a massive moment for the team and for the nation.

Teddy Sheringham had come on and done well and he came over to get hold of the ball and looked intent on taking it. "Teddy," I said, "it's too far for you. I'm taking it." I wasn't trying to be rude; I just knew, from playing with him at United, that Teddy was better from closer range. I knew this was the perfect distance for me, and for some reason I was sure that I was going to score.

Teddy did his bit by placing himself in the wall and preventing the keeper from seeing the flight of the ball, and the rest is history. I have watched the clip of that goal again and again. I must have worn out the video but I have gone over and over the technique because on that occasion I got it just right.

Here, that practice ethos is so vital. All the great players will tell you that they don't just turn up on a Saturday and produce the goods. The hard work is on the training ground and that's where I, from a very young age, worked and worked to improve my technique, especially when it came to free kicks.

"BENDING A BALL AROUND A WALL AND TRYING TO PUT IT INTO THE TOP CORNER WAS FASCINATING TO ME."

I remember during the 1998 World Cup I was feeling quite down. I had been left out of the starting lineup for the two opening group games and was more than a little frustrated. Before our final group match, though, having finished training, I went out on my own and took a bagful of balls. It was a scorching hot day in France, and so with just a tank on and my favorite hip-hop blaring out of the stereo, I struck ball after ball at the goal. It helped clear my head as well as perfect my technique.

Thank God I did. I was picked for that last game against Colombia and scored our first goal with—you've guessed it—a long-range free kick. I told you good practice makes perfect.

When the ball is in play, I have, over the years, spent a lot of my time bending the ball into the box at high speed and with a lot of swerve. From free kicks, therefore, I have the opportunity to use those exact techniques, but this time I am going for a goal and can shoot, unchallenged, in my own time.

Even today, you will find me after training, practicing and practicing free kicks. I feel I have reached a stage in my career where I can test the keeper with most free kicks that I take, but I know that without practice those standards will drop and I can still improve.

When I was a kid I loved trying to score. Bending the ball around a wall and trying to put it into the top corner was fascinating to me. I wouldn't say I was always good at it, but with practice you get better. People ask me exactly how I bend the ball, and while I do realize how it's done, it's become quite natural and something that is hard to explain.

I always had free kicks at United. Every now and then Ryan Giggs would take one from me, but that was rare. When I moved to Real Madrid, a club with so many free-kick specialists, I had to get used to waiting my turn. There are so many players in the squad wanting to try their luck, and once you've had one, you may have a long wait before your next chance. No wonder I haven't scored as many in Spain!

Approach the ball at an acute angle. I often look like I'm even coming at the ball from the side, but you can practice running at it from approximately 45 degrees.

Take a good run up, making your last stride before impact a long one (1).

Plant the non-striking foot firmly on the ground, again keeping it not too close to the ball, but not too far away (2).

Lean back slightly to ensure the ball gets up.

Wrap the foot around the ball off-center with the front inside of the foot (3). This generates swerve and spin, as you want the ball to get up over the wall but down quickly to test the keeper.

Get that ball over the wall. It's a waste when you hit the wall.

Ensure plenty of pace on the ball by getting your foot through it and following through (4).

Aim for either corner. When practicing, get used to trying different techniques and practice taking the free kicks from all areas outside the penalty box.

Your teammates can help in several ways. Like Teddy Sheringham with me in 2001, they can place themselves in the defensive wall and impede the keeper's vision until the last moment. They can also act as decoys and run at the ball as if it is they who will strike it. They run over the ball, confusing the keeper and allowing you a strike at the goal.

FREE-KICK TECHNIQUE_

1

2

3

4

My free-kick technique has become second nature to me now, but you just can't beat the feeling when you take a good one.

"EVEN TODAY, YOU WILL FIND ME AFTER TRAINING, PRACTICING AND PRACTICING FREE KICKS."

3

4

PENALTIES_

Penalties look like the easiest things in the world, don't they? Twelve yards out, only the keeper in between you and the goal—you should put it away, shouldn't you? Well, yes, I suppose you should, but it's never that easy.

My advice when taking a penalty is always make up your mind where you want to put the ball and don't change it. Ask most players and they will tell you they have missed most penalties because at the last minute they changed their minds, lost concentration, and messed up their kick.

Pick your spot, keep your eye on the ball, and ensure a nice, firm contact. You don't have to blast it —although many people like to—but ensure your contact is a good one, even if you are placing it in the corner.

My most famous penalty and perhaps the goal that gave me the most pleasure was against Argentina in the 2002 World Cup in Japan. Of course, I'd had a bad time against the Argentinians four years earlier, and to get a penalty that would put us one-up in a vital group game was always going to be a big moment for me and for the team.

The Argentinians did their best to delay the kick and to put me off, but I was having none of it. This was too big a moment for me to be distracted by silly mind games, so I put the ball down and began to focus. The stadium seemed silent, although I am sure the noise was electric. I concentrated on the ball before taking a few steps back. I took deep breaths, steadied myself, decided where I'd put it, and began my run up.

I was under pressure. I was England captain and this was massive. I had scored a few for United by smashing the ball down the middle while the keeper dived either way, so that's what I did this time. I made sure of that good contact, hit it as hard as I could while keeping my knee over the ball to make sure I kept it low—and in it went.

If you do miss one, don't be scared to have another go. The more you take, the more comfortable you'll become. Remember, everybody misses one at some point.

"MY ADVICE WHEN TAKING A PENALTY IS ALWAYS MAKE UP YOUR MIND WHERE YOU WANT TO PUT THE BALL, AND DON'T CHANGE IT."

Thank you for giving us the best day of our lives. I had a great day playing soccer and it was fun being a physical therapist . . . It was sad we had to go because it was wicked and fun.

Lucy

I am delighted you made this place so people who don't have the opportunity to play soccer can go there.

Mr. Singh (ten years old)

My son can't wait to come back to do another course at The Academy. He is already looking at dates. I have nothing but praise for the facilities provided, the way the course was organized, and the mutual respect between coaches and children.

Sharon, parent

David's mum, Sandra, has an active role at The Academy, including presenting medals at the end of the competitions.

I had an excellent day at The Academy. I also enjoyed playing soccer there and doing the challenges they set for us. If I went 1,000 times I'd still enjoy it.

Roxanne

I would like to send a massive thank-you from myself, staff, and Year 8 pupils. The coaches' ability to see the positives of all our children was clearly evident and goes a long way to raising the self-esteem of our pupils.

Steve, PE Coordinator

The fun part was when I was press officer and playing soccer and meeting new faces.

Courtney

My son was fortunate to be at your Academy and was so delighted to meet you. I cannot thank you enough for making my ten-year-old son's dreams come true.

Sheila, parent

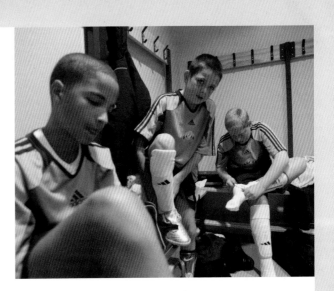

I was not only doing the thing I love most, but I was learning lots.

Daryl

I have learned a lot about what type of food to eat and how to make our bodies stronger.

Jack

It was very refreshing at the parents' induction on Monday to hear that the main ethos to The Academy is about team play and the importance of treating other players kindly.

Gill, parent

FULL NAME:
David Robert Joseph Beckham OBE

DOB:
May 2, 1975

BIRTHPLACE:
Leytonstone, England

NATIONALITY:
English

HEIGHT:
5 ft 9 in.

WEIGHT:
163 lbs

CLUB:
Real Madrid CF

POSITION:
Midfielder [R, C]

SHIRT NUMBER:
23

PREVIOUS CLUBS:
Preston North End,
Manchester United,
Real Madrid

INTERNATIONAL DEBUT:
September 1996 vs Moldova

CAPS:
94

GOALS:
17

WORLD CUPS:
France 1998, Japan-Korea 2002,
Germany 2006

TROPHIES:
UEFA Champions League (99)
Intercontinental Cup (99)
English Premier League (96, 97, 99, 00, 01, 03)
English FA Cup (96, 99)
Spanish Super Cup (03)

HONORS:
PFA Young Player of the Year (97)
UEFA Champions League Footballer of the Year (99)

- Fifth most capped England player of all time
- Only Englishman to have scored in three successive World Cup Finals
- As of December 2005, one of only four players (and the only Englishman) to have appeared in over 100 Champions League matches
- Finished runner-up European Footballer of the Year 1999 and FIFA World Player of The Year in 1999 and 2001
- BBC Sports Personality of the Year in 2001
- Opened Commonwealth Games in Manchester in 2002
- Awarded OBE for services to soccer in 2003
- Appointed as UNICEF goodwill ambassador in 2005
- Played prominent role in London's successful bid for 2012 Olympics

TOTAL APPEARANCES THROUGHOUT CAREER: **662**
TOTAL GOALS THROUGHOUT CAREER: **117**

Season	Team	L'gue	LEAGUE App	LEAGUE Goal	OTHER App	OTHER Goal
94-95	Preston North End	3	5	2	-	-
94-95	Manchester United	P	4	0	6	1
95-96	Manchester United	P	33	7	7	1
96-97	Manchester United	P	36	8	13	4
97-98	Manchester United	P	37	9	13	2
98-99	Manchester United	P	34	6	21	3
99-00	Manchester United	P	31	6	17	3
00-01	Manchester United	P	30	6	15	0
01-02	Manchester United	P	28	11	15	5
02-03	Manchester United	P	31	6	21	4
03-04	Real Madrid	P	32	3	15	4
04-05	Real Madrid	P	30	4	8	-
05-06	Real Madrid	P	32	3	14	2
Total Club			**363**	**71**	**165**	**29**

"Other"–includes other La Liga, FA, and UEFA competitions

INTERNATIONAL SUMMARY:

Season	Team	App	Goals
96-97	England	9	0
97-98	England	9	1
98-99	England	4	0
99-00	England	12	0
00-01	England	8	3
01-02	England	12	3
02-03	England	6	4
03-04	England	12	2
04-05	England	9	3
05-06	England	13	1
Total Internationals		**94**	**17**

Soccer stats as of July 2006

DAVID BECKHAM FACTFILE_